THE WHEEL OF ETERNITY

Also by Helen Greaves

THE DISSOLVING VEIL
TESTIMONY OF LIGHT

HELEN GREAVES

The Wheel of Eternity

SAFFRON WALDEN
THE C.W. DANIEL COMPANY LIMITED

FIRST PUBLISHED
IN GREAT BRITAIN IN 1974
BY NEVILLE SPEARMAN LIMITED
112 WHITFIELD STREET, LONDON WIP 6DP

ISBN 0 85435 192 2

Reprinted 1988

To M.J.

for help when I felt I could not go on

Produced by Ennisfield Ltd., London

CONTENTS

FOREWORD

by

The Rev. K. G. Cuming, M.R.C.S., L.R.C.P.

It is a privilege to have been asked to write a foreword to this beautiful book. Readers of Mrs Greaves' other books, *The Dissolving Veil* and *Testimony of Light*, will know that she has a great gift for putting across profound spiritual teaching in eminently readable language. Not only that, but she is endowed with a finely sensitive ability to receive and transmit thought communications, telepathically received, from discarnate souls on different levels of spiritual evolution.

Her gift, however, is deeper and wider than mere telepathy, for it has in it a touch of almost mystical awareness of Light and Beauty in the radiance that streams forth from spiritually advanced souls; as well as the power to perceive the darker aspects and powerful emotions that surround the environment of souls in the darkness of the Shadow Lands.

Readers of *Testimony of Light* will remember that in it, Mrs Greaves recorded the experiences of a great soul, Frances Banks (Sister Frances Mary of the Community of the Resurrection, Grahamstown, South Africa), after her passing to the Higher Life. Thousands have been comforted, in their bereavement, by that book.

In this new book, Mrs Greaves has indeed been called to be in herself, a 'Channel into Light'. For, in her little cottage in a

Sussex village, she has been used by Higher Powers as a means of bringing the light of understanding to earthbound souls imprisoned by their own ignorance and selfishness. Little did Mrs Greaves realise, when she first came to live in that cottage, that she would be deeply and personally involved, in an emotional, psychic, and spiritual sense, in the life of a former inhabitant of the cottage, technically 'dead' but quite unaware of the fact, as are so many souls today.

The story tells of a triangle of human relationships, with its roots in the tragic life in this world, and its dramatic working out of the consequences in the Shadow Lands of the next world. The arrogant, domineering mistress, hating her idiot bastard son, and enslaving and despising the old woman who was her maid, is the apex of a human triangle of love-hate relationships.

One is tempted to quote Bishop Trevor Huddleston's phrase and say that in this story of conditions in a part of the next life, there is 'Nought for your comfort.' But this is not entirely true, and would indeed be quite misleading. For, though the spiritual lesson that Christ taught, that 'As a man sows, so shall he also reap', is driven home with relentless power, yet through all the working out of this drama there shines the Grace of God and the Power of Love to redeem any situation, however dark.

There is much in this book that will upset people who have a cosy, sentimental idea of Divine Forgiveness, as well as those who interpret the doctrine of the Vicarious Atonement as implying that you can do what you like in this life and as long as you say you are sorry, then Christ's death on the Cross will make it all right for you in the next world. It would seem that death-bed repentances are not the whole answer, only a beginning. They do not ensure, as some church people and also some clergy seem to think, that you will 'wake up in the arms of Jesus'.

The more one studies the many purported communications from the Life Beyond, especially those that relate details of life in the Astral Planes and the Shadow Lands (the Lower Astral), the more one realises their consistency of accounts from differing, independent sources. They all demonstrate the same abiding spiritual truth—that forgiveness is not 'let-off-ness', that all debts must be repaid, and all wrongs worked out and put right. It becomes abundantly clear in this story that by our harmful, selfish actions in this life, by the wrong we do to others whether from ignorance or selfishness, we create, quite literally, our own 'hells' in the next life. We also learn that hatred is as powerful a force to bind people together as is Love.

So, although God undoubtedly forgives us, and we may forgive others who have wronged us, we are still tied to those we have wronged, until they forgive us. No wonder Jesus said, 'Judge not, that ye be not judged.' As the Mistress prayed the Lord's Prayer in her agony of remorse, she added the thought 'May they forgive me, who has trespassed against them.' A sobering thought, indeed.

One is reminded of the old story of the 'Hell-fire and Damnation' Scottish minister, denouncing from his pulpit the wicked ways of his congregation, and thundering,

'And it will be no use then for ye to go doon on yer knees and say "Lord, Lord, we didna ken!" For the Lord in His Infinite Maircy will look doon upon ye from Heaven, and He'll say to ye, "Weel, ye ken noo!" '

Ignorance of Divine Law, it appears, is no excuse. Perfect Love must embrace not only Divine Mercy, but likewise Divine Justice.

Yet through the whole book, shining with a golden glow that softens all harshness, and illumines all darkness of spirit, is Divine Love. It manifests in the loving forgiveness of the Boy for his ignorant, proud and haughty mother, the love of the old woman for the Boy she had looked after, and above all the shining radiance, the gentle wisdom of the Brother of Light, who guides the whole drama through to its logical conclusion within the Perfect Law of Divine Love, the liberation of self-enchained souls from their bondage and their progress into the Light.

K. G. CUMING,
Chairman,
Churches' Fellowship for Psychical and Spiritual Studies.

FOREWORD

by Paul Beard

Extra-sensory perception is often thought to be an odd or way-out faculty, little related to everyday experience. As a result, many people's approach is to write it all off as nonsense. Alternatively, people attribute to such perception powers so inclusive as to fall little short of the miraculous! Genuine extra-sensory perception is a human faculty which really, of course, lies in a much more moderate area, away from such extremes.

One of the charms of this book, written by a non-professional sensitive, lies in its candour and obvious truthfulness as a record, and in revealing how natural and in accord with normal human feelings and motives the use of this faculty is.

In her narrative, Mrs Greaves shows very clearly how extra-sensory perception has nothing to do with the magical, but is the result of a trained enhancement of perception, which in order to be able to operate does so at times when the sensitive is, so to speak, in closest harmony within herself. One is reminded of Mozart's description of how he produced his work; he did so when 'feeling most himself'. Similarly, Mrs Greaves, it is clear, needs to be most herself in order for the necessary step-up, or intensification of consciousness to take place.

Another important factor will be noticed. This is that almost invariably the initiative for making contact lies with her 'visitors' and not with Mrs Greaves herself. Whilst she has to be attuned, this will not of itself produce her visitors. She must await their coming. She cannot 'call them up'—a feat often attributed to sensitives by those ignorant of the subject, who then often go on to censure the sensitive for thus doing something which no sensitive can do because it is quite contrary to the realities of the situation!

Sensitive readers will notice too that the onset of her E.S.P. as described by Mrs Greaves has a different texture, so to speak, according to who her visitor is. Clearly those who participate in it at the other end of the line qualify it simply as a result of their own nature, and influence its particular character on that occasion. Thus when the old servant comes, Mrs Greaves does not need to attune herself so keenly as when her visitor is the Brother; she does not have to reach to the furthest stretch of her perceptions as is necessary when the latter is present. Even after doing so, it would seem she is also aware that there are in the Brother's being levels of awareness which, as a person in a physical body, she is prevented from reaching. One of the most convincing factors in the book is this evidence for these important differences in spiritual level between one visitor and another, and which, in their impact on the sensitive, call for different levels of response from her. These differences are seen also to determine the environment in which each communicator is able to live.

This book, therefore, adds a valuable sheaf of experience to the growing store of accounts through minds of integrity, of the alterations of consciousness which accompany life after death, which it is clear are consequent upon the way life has been lived whilst still on earth. These relationships of cause and effect, as seen in such communications, indeed form an important subject for study and I welcome this valuable contribution accordingly.

PAUL BEARD,
President, the College
of Psychic Studies.

PREFACE

This story may be read as an allegory, as an imaginary tale, as inspiration, as a thesis on archetypes in man, or as a telepathic record from Mind to mind of an actual happening out of time and space.

To the writer, this last statement is fact, for in every chapter of this drama, she participated, not only as recorder, but as one with those who were living through their deep emotional experiences.

If we realise and accept the precept that we are all united in the one life which we call God, then it must follow that every human being is related to every other expression of the Divine . . . not the dense physical form, but the soul, the mind and the energy. Response, therefore, is made by the individual, consciously or unconsciously, to other minds, human, astral or spiritual, according to his knowledge, experience and progress. This consciousness or response, which we call telepathy, is, among other developments which will shift the emphasis from outer to inner man, one of the significant techniques to be perfected in the coming new age. It will bring a new meaning and a deeper purpose to the evolution of man, and, on a higher level of awareness, initiate a balancing of cause and effect and further revelation into the mysteries of experience and interpretation. For, hitherto, man has rarely examined the conscious motive of life. He needs a spiritual revaluation to prepare him for the understanding of himself, his nature, and his heritage.

These are the challenges, which confront us in the fast-changing life on this planet. But, whatever these revolutionary patterns entail, still the age-old truth of love and wisdom in the Divine Plan and Purpose will prevail, and the evolutionary process of man's spiritual responsibility for his own acts will proceed.

This story was the way in which I was shown the working out of individual and collective cause and effect. This was the channel into light, which was revealed.

May it bring light to those who read.

Sussex, 1973.

LEAD, KINDLY LIGHT

Lead, kindly Light, amid the encircling gloom,
    Lead Thou me on;
The night is dark, and I am far from home,
    Lead Thou me on. . . .

So long Thy power has blest me, sure it still
    Will lead me on,
O'er moor and fen, o'er crag and torrent till
    The night is gone;
And with the morn those Angel faces smile,
Which I have loved long since, and lost awhile.

                 John Henry Newman

CHAPTER ONE

The Cottage

In the Autumn of 1971, I moved into a tiny sixteenth-century cottage in a Sussex village, one in a terrace of dwellings, which had, I imagine, originally been the homes of farm labourers. These dwellings had thick walls, hung tiles, and were low-ceilinged and oak-beamed. During this twentieth century, the terrace had fallen into dilapidation, and was scheduled for eventual destruction.

But (as I was told by a local shopkeeper), the old cottages were saved by an architect of vision and skill, who bought up the entire street, and proceeded to modernise it.

If this little cottage is a sample of his work, then, indeed, he must be congratulated, not only for preserving old buildings, but also for his harmonious and unobtrusive mingling of the old and the new. For the rooms are still low, with dark oak beams crossing the ceilings, the windows are enlarged yet still in keeping, the great inglenook in the sitting room, with the weathered oak beam above it, makes an interesting alcove for books and television screen; and at the back of the house the paved courtyard has sufficient earth-beds for the planting of shrubs and flowers to make a pleasant patio. But modernisation has built on an up-to-date kitchen with neon lighting, capacious cupboards, and a sliding glass door to separate it from the sitting room. At one end of the long parlour, an open curved staircase leads to a landing above, a modern bathroom, an attractive L-shaped bedroom, also with a sliding door, and above that, reached by a miniature spiral staircase, an attic guest room. All the walls, woodwork and ceiling strips between the beams are white, and the whole dwelling emphasises clever functional planning in an old world atmosphere.

This is the cottage of my story. Before I moved in, I was informed that 'it had an atmosphere'. Indeed, I soon discovered that it had. When furnishing was completed, and friends invited to view, they invariably fell in love with the cottage (as I had done!), and remarked on the peaceful and comforting feeling that seemed to be part of it. To this I agreed, and I settled into my new home with happy anticipations. I had, then, no clue to any work to be done there, nor any pre-cognition of the strange events that would take place in that cosy sitting room before many moons had risen and set. I was entirely happy and at peace with my work, my books, music and television, and the visits of friends.

I must have been settled in for less than a few weeks, however, when something did happen, which startled me, though it caused no fear. I was sitting before the electric fire in the inglenook, reading, when my attention was drawn from my book by a strange feeling of apprehension . . . a disturbing vibration as of a stranger watching me. Startled, I looked up. Immediately, I became 'aware' of an old woman. She was sitting in the armchair opposite, and she was staring at me with curiosity and interest. She was dressed (or appeared so to be), in a long black frock, tight over the bosom, and full in the floor-length skirt. An immaculate white apron with a bib protected the dress front. Under the severely brushed-back grey hair, the little wizened face with its large sombre eyes regarded me with a sort of 'other-worldly' expression, which immediately marked her out as a recluse . . . the person who minds her own business, and expects you to respect it. She had a thin tight mouth, as if all her life she had had to button up her words, and so had been flung in upon herself; and it was this, and her odd 'lost' expression, which made me take notice of her.

Is this a ghost, I asked myself? And I admit for a moment I was a little scared, for I had never seen what could be termed a 'ghost' before. Always I had been aware of the appearance of a departed spirit, but that had always been an inner seeing.

This was almost objective. I closed my eyes, wondering what would happen next. Was the cottage haunted? Nothing happened. Cautiously, I looked again.

She was still there. She eyed me as closely and with as much interest as if I was a visitor from outer space. As I looked at her, our glances met and held. Then her tight little mouth seemed to relax into a half-smile of welcome. Immediately all fear left me. This was no haunting ghost, I told myself, but a little 'lost' soul, a pathetic lonely little soul. I began to wonder what she wanted, and whether this feeling of sympathy communicated itself to her I could not tell, but without any preamble, I found myself able to pick up her thoughts by telepathy.

The poor old soul was not even musing upon my identity, nor speculating on my reason for being in the cottage. I could feel no antipathy; she seemed to have accepted me without question; indeed, I had the strange impression that she was glad to have me there for company, as I recalled that the place had been empty for long. Suddenly and distinctly, I knew that she was telling me her name. Afterwards I wrote it down (but have not thought about it since). Then she explained her right to be in the cottage. This had been her 'very own' home, she communicated through the mind; she had lived here by herself, 'since my Mistress died', which I gathered was some years before. I felt an unspoken plea that I was not going to take her home away from her, was I? At this I hastened to give out the thought that there was room for both of us, and she accepted this without any demur. Shy at first, slowly she imparted facts about her life, as if she was still living it. She had been a servant for years, she told me, in a large house not far away, and she made a gesture in the direction.

The poor old soul is earthbound, I thought; she cannot know that she is not still in this material world. How long has she been in this half-state? By the antique look of her dress, which is her thought-form of herself, she must have sojourned here for years. She is a hangover from the end of the last century.

Even as I decided these facts, the old woman was gone. She seemed to slip away into nothingness, leaving me wondering whether I had imagined her. The 'visitation' puzzled me, but as she did not return for some weeks, I began to dismiss the whole incident. Perhaps, I told myself, I had been overtired with all the efforts of moving, and had fallen asleep and dreamed it all.

It was not until near Christmas, and the long dark days of December made fireside evenings so enjoyable, that I had another visit from my fellow-occupant.

It was one evening, early in the month, when I was sitting in my usual chair by the fireside, listening to music from the radio, and mending a long, modern necklace, made up of thin, linking chains, not silver but silvered, of which one strand had been broken. I was very engrossed in this, and was not aware of any change in the atmosphere, and it was not until I looked up that I 'saw' I had a visitor. The little old woman was in the chair opposite me, watching me with the greatest interest and concentration.

I went quietly on with my work, as though I was still alone, but I was certain that both of us knew that we were in contact. Then I realised that she was longing to talk. Out of the corner of my eye, I saw her smooth down her white apron (a characteristic gesture I was sure!) and then look directly at me, and 'speak' inside herself.

'My Mistress had a chain like that,' she began. 'Only with thicker links; solid *and* silver.'

I found myself smiling inwardly. '*Real* silver?'

Her mouth pursed into a button. 'Real silver! My Mistress was rich!'

'Ah!' I thought, amused at her pride in another's wealth.

'Hers come to 'er waist. It had a great locket, big as a crown it was, hanging from it.'

I wanted to maintain the conversation. 'Like a great medallion?' I prompted.

There was no response. Perhaps the word was not in her vocabulary.

'With writing on one side. Mistress set great store by it. Never was without them . . . the chain and the locket. Wore 'em with all her dresses, all them stiff silks she liked so much. . . .'

'Your Mistress had smart dresses?'

She seemed to sniff at being asked such a question. 'Elegant, they was. The Mistress was handsome an' elegant. I remember she always wore silk when she was young. When the Master, 'er husband died, folks thought she'd marry again. But she never. The young Master too, had been drowned in the pond, and. . . .'

'Drowned!' I couldn't check my interest. 'How sad!'

Maybe I had expressed the wrong reaction. Maybe I had taken the confidence too literally. Maybe my old woman reacted to the idea of sadness . . . or death! I had no way of knowing then.

For she was gone.

When I opened my eyes (for oddly enough I close them to 'hear'), the chair opposite was vacant, the music was over, and a radio voice droned on in a talk which I had not even heard.

I had a premonition that this was going to be a serial in many parts. And so it turned out.

CHAPTER TWO

Visitors

I was often conscious of the old woman in my sitting room. She would come and sit in the chair, curled up like a cat that has come back to its warm hearth. She seemed to be quite content just to be in company with me, and there was not very much I received from her in those first visits. But we were in harmony, and that was to be a beginning for the work to come later.

It was quite obvious that she enjoyed my fireplace, though I soon realised that to her, the inglenook still housed the old iron stove, which must have imparted an impression of warmth and comfort. Her vision could not perceive that the chimney was now blocked up, and that the nook was furnished with a radiant electric fire (though she would scarcely know what that was), and a television screen, which would have been all the more inscrutable, to her. In her thought-world, she still believed that the wood stove burned, that the pots bubbled on the hobs, and that the room was small and dark, as it must once have been. What she thought of me, I did not know, but she was not afraid of me. She was pathetic in her longing for company, and had evidently accepted me as a tenant. She did nothing as far as I could see, but sit. Whether she thought or not, I had no way of discovering, but at times I would pick up an idea from her mind. Usually it was about her life, about the great house where she had spent a life of service, about the arrogance and cruelty of her mistress, and sometimes (but not often, for this must have been a sad memory), about the boy, the young Master, who in his early teens had lost his life in the pond.

And then, one evening, she burst out at me, almost as though she had to confide her anxieties; and this time, I kept my feelings under control and expressed no emotion, remembering that she had fled away from sympathy before.

It was after we had sat together in silent communion two or three times. I noticed that she was restless, smoothing down her apron, and twisting her hands together. The poor old thing is worrying, I thought. Immediately, her mind communicated with mine.

'It's the Boy I'm wondering about,' she fussed. 'Poor Sonny, he was weak in the head. Didn't have no real life, he didn't. *She* couldn't bear him near 'er. There was a time she wanted to put 'im away. But the old Master wouldn't 'ear of it. . . .'

Whether she was aware that I was tuned in on this, or not, I did not know. I kept my thoughts as serene as possible, and listened.

It is a strange, almost eerie, experience to be hearing the secret thoughts of another individual, especially when I was quite aware that this was a disembodied spirit, locked up and earthbound in her own small world of illusion. Yet at the time (though I cannot explain this, and it will sound a contradiction in terms!) it seemed natural enough. But her next thought really stunned me!

'Not that the old Master knew much. 'E was too easy-going with 'er, and she knew 'ow to get round him. Would 'e have kept the Boy in the house, if he'd known all I knew? That the Boy weren't 'is own flesh and blood . . . a fly-by-night, a rompin-the-'ay child of an 'andsome gardener wot come to work for us for a while. Oh, the Mistress was proud an' self-willed. Reckon she had suspicion of me knowing, but I never give 'er that satisfaction . . . so she 'ad to keep me on. And the poor Boy. I tried to make up to 'im for his mother. I wonder now if he ever knew. . . ?'

Here was a story in a nutshell, a sad, pathetic tale from the memories of a simple soul. It was poignant, and it was very real. What a lot I had learned in a few words about old half-forgotten sorrows, about loves and hates, about deceits and, thankfully, about compassion. As I was not certain that the old soul meant me to know her secrets, I made no comment. And after a while, she left me.

But the next evening, when she was there by the inglenook, she must have decided that I knew all about it, for she re-iterated, 'I was fond of 'im, I was. An' he trusted me. An idiot. It must 'ave been terrible for him. I wonder wot happened to him?'

With gentle deliberateness, I sent out the thought, 'But he was drowned in the pond, wasn't he?'

She looked bemused for a while. Then she accepted it.

'Ah! Drowned, so 'e was. Goin' in after a bird, I remember. An' no-one to tell 'im it was deep in the middle. Poor Sonny, 'ad no life . . . and now 'e's dead. . . . It was 'er fault . . . 'er fault. 'Eartless, that's wot she was. . . .'

She sat on for a while. Then she got up. I saw her at the inglenook as if she was mending her fire; then she was gone. But her story stayed with me.

Old half-forgotten wounds! I couldn't remember where I had read that . . . but now I knew how they lived on in the minds and memories.

How fatally true are those lines from the *Rubaiyat* of Omar Khayyam.

> *The Moving Finger writes, and having writ,*
> *Moves on; nor all thy Piety nor Wit*
> *Shall lure it back to cancel half a line.*
> *Nor all thy Tears wash out a Word of it.*

I pondered on the reason why I had been entrusted with this story. What had it to do with me? Apart from welcoming the old servant as a friend, there was little, I decided, that I could do.

But I was to learn differently; and that before much time had passed.

January 18th

Today an interesting piece of evidence came my way unsought, and therefore all the more valuable.

This morning a lady called on me, announced herself as a neighbour, and came in for a short time in order to invite me to tea at her house and therefore become better acquainted. She was charming, and friendly. She seemed quite knowledgeable about the village, where, she told me, she had lived for several years. She enquired if I knew the history of the place and when I said I did not, she told me about the original iron-mines of Sussex, and about the 'Hammer ponds' that were once such a feature of the village.* I was immediately interested. I had not heard of these stretches of water for cooling the hot iron ore. So I asked whether there were many of these ponds, and where they were situated. She told me much concerning them, but there was one in particular, she said, not far from us, and she described its position.

It was in the place where my 'old lady' had described 'her' pond! The pond where the Boy had been drowned. I was suddenly warm with excitement, though I refrained from appearing too eager. But here was corroboration. Here was proof that:

a. there was a pond:
b. that the earthbound entity knew of that pond and had pointed in its direction, and
c. that it had not all been a figment of my imagination.

---

* Iron was certainly produced in the Ashdown Forest in Roman days. The first casting of iron cannon was done in 1540 at Oldlands in the parish of Buxted. Thereafter Sussex had the complete monopoly of iron gun casting for two centuries, becoming known as the 'Black Country' of England.

The site of an iron-works was chosen near to beds of ore and to some available water power. Artificial ponds were generally constructed by dams of earth against the stream, the head of water so obtained driving a wheel connected to the machinery of the hammer or furnace. In 1606 there were nearly 140 hammers and furnaces of iron.

I began to be more than interested. Here was just not idle gossip of a garrulous old soul clinging to the past; here was the opening chapter of a saga, in which I knew that I was to be involved, whether I wanted to be or not.

And so it came to pass. I had not long to wait.

CHAPTER THREE

The Vision

One Sunday morning in January, after a relaxed and gentle meditation, I was swept into another state of consciousness, indeed a new world. This was a state in which I heard, I saw, I knew. I found myself a part of a living tableau, deeply involved with it, as the tableau was broken up into varied scenes, and the scenes into a dramatic drama.

For nearly two hours (checked later by the clock), I remained in this extended consciousness. I seemed to be a living sentient Mind, separated from the body. There was no time; past, present, and future were all one, for I lived in past actions, forgotten dramas, which were all strange to me, as well as 'taking part' in pre-cognitive future happenings. It seemed, then, that there was no definite recognisable division between that past history in the heavier matter of the earth plane, and ethereal future action in the lighter plane of the Spirit. It was the most momentous example of being 'caught up into the Spirit' which I had ever experienced.

If I say that I took part in a re-enacted story, I mean just that. As I lay with my eyes closed, utterly engrossed, the drama unfolded and, as in a play, one act led on to another and finally to the climax. It was all tightly knit, and entirely plausible. The actors pulsated with life, and human passion rang through it all . . . and in a strange way I felt myself a part of it . . . as indeed I was to be, yet at that time I had no notion of such a possibility. But as days and weeks passed, and other 'visitors' from a future life communicated with me, this painful saga of three lives resolved itself into such a tremendous Purpose as to stir my very soul to its depths.

This 'one-ness' of Life which, that morning, was brought home so clearly to me, was the whole purpose of my participation in the drama. Soon I realised that the appearance of the old serving woman in the cottage had been the curtain raiser to a new consciousness and a task which I could not refuse. Later, when I was able to bring my reasoning mind into the examination of this phenomenon, I was able to sift this vital interplay between mind and Mind, and mind and matter. It was all part of the same Power, the Alpha and Omega of existence . . . Spirit.

There is no separation between human and human, between human and animal, between human and vegetable. We live in the fallacy of separation, because we are 'closed up' in our bodies and re-act only to the five senses; because what I think of as 'me' is something of flesh and bone, packed up in skin like a parcel wrapped in paper. But that skin covering is like Thysbe's wall. It only *appears* to separate us from others. About these very bodies is a 'radiation', an interplay that attracts or repels. We 'bump into' each other far oftener than by physical contact. We are in touch emotionally, mentally, spiritually far more than we know. Why? Because we are all One in this divine Creative Force, in God. These two hours of increased awareness and vision, and the subsequent 'contacts' with entities who no longer inhabited the house of flesh convinced me, once and for all, that there is *no separation*, even by death. The casting off of the body means little. Matter is merely energy in a certain state of vibration and does not alter the Mind, which persists and, at the first stages after death, much in the way it did whilst in a 'skin-house'. By this I mean that the mind seems to carry on, after the falling away of the physical body, in its accustomed groove; i.e. dully, stubbornly, blindly (as in the case of my old woman in the cottage who refused to recognise that she had left the material world); or, angrily, resentfully (as a future communicator revealed); or gloriously uniting with its soul, and *becoming* One with the Power of Good, as I was to witness in a future session.

Everything is One, of one Substance, one Power, one Energy.

This is not a new statement; it has been repeated and affirmed in the religions of the world throughout the ages. Yet, in this twentieth century of the miraculous in scientific development we still grope for an answer. We still choose to ignore the fact that by 'tuning in' to this One-ness, we would become whole in body, mind and spirit; we would live fully here and now, less apt to make so many disastrous mistakes; and we would accept physical death for what it is, a state of mental and spiritual progress, instead of the gloomy end to the illusive 'joys' of life.

Here, then, follows the aftermath of the story in which I have become involved. Can we learn from it? Can we even afford to ignore the implications of a Divine Plan for all? Dare we, in our ignorance, seek to mitigate the force of Love which acts as the God-Power to bring all souls into peace, progress and Light? Can we not realise that our very acceptance of the limitation of matter closes away from us the vast potentialities of the soul, and the knowledge that could lead to finer lives and to happier experiences here and Hereafter?

If this astral drama, which is the aftermath of these lives communicated to me by the transference of thought from another level of consciousness, can teach us anything, or if it can awaken in the readers a spark of love and hope, or kindle a new faith in the perfect Plan and merciful justice of spiritual Law, then I shall feel justified in having imparted this vision to sceptics as well as to believers, to the curiosity-seeker as much as to the awakened ego. My work will not have been in vain.

CHAPTER FOUR

The Boy

During the long January evenings, I was often aware of the old servant. She was no trouble; she brought no bad vibrations, and I never once thought of the cottage as 'haunted', as I had heard it described. My visitor and I were on good terms; all she seemed to need was company. But during those visits, she did impart to me quite a lot of information about her life as a maid in the big house. Indeed, she lived in the past; it was more real to her than her present state.

Thus I came to know all about the Family (you could almost *feel* the capital letter), and the strange story which had been part of the vision of that Sunday morning. She talked more about the boy than the others, and it was plain to see that she had been very fond of him. I gathered that he was a silent child, partly because he had great difficulty in putting his thoughts and words together into even simple conversation, and partly because his nature was solitary too. She said he would play contentedly for hours with some simple jar, screwing the top off and on with great concentration, though not always managing to accomplish this successfully. He was an obedient boy, too, not given to tantrums and, she stressed, very affectionate. And he worshipped his arrogant good-looking mother!

The story, as I pieced it together from the old woman's reminiscences and the scenes in the vision, was an ordinary-enough tale, yet with such moving undertones that sometimes I found it difficult to banish it from my mind. My sympathy for the poor boy grew. I, too, wondered about him. What a wasted life it seemed!

The mistress, it appeared, did not marry until in her late twenties, which was surprising, as she was both rich and handsome. Then she took for husband a man much older than she, and he seemed to be under her thumb from the very beginning. She ran the house and estate; he was merely an appendage. But they kept up appearances. There were no children, until the boy arrived some years after the marriage, when his mother was in her middle thirties. A good-looking young man from heaven knows where one day applied for work and was interviewed by the mistress, who, without references or any other palaver, took him on as an under-gardener. How much of what the old woman said she knew was true, I am in no position to judge. Suffice it that the wandering gardener was evidently seduced by a passion-hungry woman, and there was a short-lived intense affair between them, of which the complacent husband appeared completely unaware. The result was that the young man took himself off after working for six months, and was never heard of again. Later, the mistress' son was born, an unwanted child who soon showed signs of a maladjusted mind and an uncontrolled body.

The boy's mother could not bear him near her; he was both an embarrassment and an intrusion into her ordered life. She abandoned him to the care of the servants, so that my visitor assumed the role of confidante and protector. She told me that the boy loved the birds and animals and had no fear of any of them. He would converse in a funny guttural language for the kitchen garden and the thrushes, blackbirds and tits in the hours with the swans on the lake, as well as with the hens in orchard. And, strangely enough, it was his love for the birds which caused his death. He was fifteen at the time, a big gang-ling youth with good features but a vacant expression. Usually, my old woman told me, when he wandered about the grounds she was watching him, or there was a gardener close by; but on this particular spring morning he must have dodged out by himself. It appears that a blackbird with a broken wing had taken refuge on a branch of a tree overhanging the pond. The boy caught sight of it, as it fluttered down on to the water, and lay there helpless. He, innocent of danger, waded out to help it and stepped into a deep hole. He could not swim and by the time the gardener saw him his body was floating face downwards and his half-life was over. My old woman had never completely forgiven herself for not having been beside him to raise the alarm.

But it was the mother's attitude which riled her. The mistress took it calmly . . . 'never shed a tear, she didn't', and after the funeral gave orders for everything of her son's to be removed and destroyed. It was a deliberate action to cast away the part of her life which she had hated. She was then about fifty years old and her husband much older. The winter following the tragedy, the husband caught pneumonia and died and she was left alone, except for the servants, in the big house. After that, according to her maid, she became tyrannical, resentful, and her health deteriorated. For the last ten years of her life she was practically an invalid, with heart trouble and other maladies. She died alone and with an expression of terror on her face that seemed to have burnt itself into the memory of the old servant. Some while later, when relatives took over the house, old Nan (as she once told me she was called) was offered this tiny cottage, then shabby and dark, as a home. To the old woman, who had served others, without gratitude, all her life, it was like heaven. It was plain to understand why she could not leave; no orthodox heaven could possibly be a greater joy.

This was the story that came, bit by bit, from the mind and memories of this poor earthbound soul. It was real, it was poignant and it all seemed so hopeless, until I recalled that, from my vision, I was to be part of a future . . . if there could be a future!

One evening in late January I was watching a television programme when my 'inner senses' informed me that there was a change in the atmosphere, a heightening (I use this word for want of a better) of the vibrations. Instinctively, I knew that I was not alone and I looked at the opposite corner for my usual visitor, the old servant.

She was not there. But now I had lost interest in the television screen. This was something far more important . . . far more wonderful even than the modern 'miracle' of television. I switched off the set, resumed my seat, closed my eyes, and endeavoured to calm my mind whilst I waited. Slowly, my consciousness lifted. On to my inner sight flashed the figures of two Visitors from another World. It was quite obvious to me that I could never have seen them with my physical eyes, so different were they from the poor earthbound entity who thought she shared my cottage.

They *shone*. I can explain it no other way. To me, the room was filled with Light and pervaded with such a sweetness and love that I was aware of tears in my eyes.

Slowly, the forms became more distinct. There were two and they seemed linked together in some inexplicable way. They were young men, though one appeared little more than a youth, and the other gave the impression of wisdom and experience which came from age, yet had nothing to do with our material measurement of years. I found myself riveted on to his expression, which was one of such beauty and serenity that my first thought was 'god-like'. Light seemed to emerge from him, or he to emerge from light . . . I could not distinguish which. His robe, which was white, gleamed as though light flowed through it.

At last my attention was caught by the younger man. His face had a chiselled look, almost as if he was carved in marble, so perfect were his features. Yet he did not glow, as his companion did. I found myself puzzling about this, when I was interrupted by a startling thought that was shot into my mind, like a firework exploding in my consciousness.

'The Boy.' Just those two words. 'The Boy.'

I was silenced. Was this an hallucination? Immediately, my physical mind interrupted, reasoning that the Boy, of whom I had learned from the old servant, had been weak in intellect. This youth, I felt, was a soul advanced in wisdom. I must have been mistaken.

But presently I knew that the mind of this young man was

communicating with mine. Quickly I caught up pad and pen. This, I knew, must be recorded.

'I am the Boy, of whom you have heard', came the words. 'The poor creature who once lived in this neighbourhood where you now dwell. Yes, I recall that I passed from earthlife by drowning. You cannot "see" me as yet, but your Self is aware of the contact, and this has come as a surprise to you. Yes, I am the Boy, of whom the earthbound woman spoke, the son of the Mistress she served. I was a soul drawn to earth-life in a body of flesh created by the lowest physical emotions of lust and not by love. You have not, perhaps, realised that a love-body, i.e. cells joined and fused in the physical union of two who love each other, is often of superior quality to the flesh formation of a casual coupling unhallowed by tenderness? This is often so, though there are exceptions. Yet the *soul* drawn into such an ill-formed skin-house can be one of great spiritual progress, even a Saviour of the race, or a genius, or a dedicated server of mankind. Such High Beings *do* sacrifice themselves for the progress and evolution of their fellows, or for the advancement of the animal or even the vegetable world.

'Yet I came not as one of these. This Brother of Light, who stands beside me, is a starry Point in the Group to which I, as a lowly aspiring soul, belong. It was by his protection and love that I was enabled to endure the mind-prison of a defective brain in your earth-life, an incarnation which I had chosen for a special experience. Our souls were so united by love and purpose, that strength was often afforded me as by a miracle. In sleep I knew his comfort and care; in dreams I beheld his radiance, as a guardian Angel, yet my deficient mind could not retain or express this awareness. Only in the contact with birds and flowers and trees could I dimly apprehend the Love and Creative Intelligence of Divinity. I was almost mute, dumb in the physical expression of what my soul knew—I suffered. My friend, if you wish confirmation of my statements, look *with perception* into the eyes of a retarded child; there you will often perceive the imprisoned soul, longing for yet incapable of, and therefore denied, expression.

'And so with me. My mother had no natural love for me. I was both a reproach and an incubus. But the serving woman, whom you know as the "old woman in the cottage", simple, earthbound, unenlightened, *loved* me. She gave me the devotion of her soul and the work of her body. For such comfort, for such compassion, come We now to bring her Light; to free her from the dark unconsciousness and fear which have clouded her soul for some space of your earth time.

'I myself could accomplish little. But the power and wisdom of my Brother's consciousness (for he is a most advanced soul), is closer to awareness of the Christ, and therefore has an infinite potency for good. His service is dedicated rescue work for those who have temporarily lost the Way, and with his help, and yours, we can save her from her self-imposed blindness. There is fear with her, dear friend, about which you do not know as yet. But she gave unselfish love, and love is Life. Life shall be restored to her. Remember the Christ message "Love thy neighbour as thyself."

'In this release of an imprisoned soul we trust you will play your part as the scribe, the listener, the go-between 'twixt earth consciousness and soul-awareness; and as a catalyst, who is used to trigger recollection from the chain of events.

'Life, you see, is not so different in this plane from life in the earth-world. We only live more in the mind, less in the emotions; more in the consciousness of the all-pervading Spirit, and no longer confined by the weight and pressure of denser matter.

'Therefore, "Mind-Catalyst", before we withdraw our consciousness from yours, My Brother of Light bids you hold your "fellow-lodger" in the Light of prayerful thought, that of her own accord, she may confide in you those memories and fears that blot her conscience, and hold her to earth. Farewell.'

I put aside the pen and pad. The session was over. But what a session it had been! What surprise; what unexpected developments had already arisen out of telepathic communication with my old servant. The vision which had uplifted my consciousness and had illustrated this story of the Mistress, the Boy and the woman who served them, had in vague references indicated that the story had not ended. Indeed for me it seemed only now to be commencing. To say I was concerned is an understatement. Yet, as I sat on, pondering over much that had now been communicated, I could see that I had little choice about participation. I had a gift which had been fully demonstrated by Frances Banks, in *Testimony of Light*. Now I was called upon to extend that gift. *Testimony of Light*, I had been informed so often, had helped to bring faith and healing to many people. There must then be a Purpose, beyond my comprehension, in co-operating with this strange astral drama and making of it a book which would go out to the public. Any feelings I had in the matter, any natural shrinking from publicity and criticism, must be put aside, as had been done in the case of Frances' book. The old servant must be awakened to Reality, and helped on her way to her next experiences. The Boy must be allowed to fulfil his 'debt of love', the Brother of Light to bring Light into darkness and ignorance, as was his Christ Mission. I was a mere cog in the wheel, yet a cog must perform its function.

For some while I sat and considered, but again and again my thoughts went back to the beauty of that countenance of Love, and I felt held, almost as if cocooned, in a vibration of a love and peace such as I had never experienced. Before I went to bed, I knew that I was blessed indeed to be allowed to be entrusted even with this humble service. I felt that my soul had accepted this, long before my rebellious personality had received the smallest inkling concerning the work.

CHAPTER FIVE

The Boy and the Brother

'I was drowned in the pond,' continued the Boy at a later session, 'that fact your "old woman" has told you. But the truth is that I was released from a prison of the mind by the influx of water.

'There is much more in this than a bald statement of asphyxiation caused by the flooding of water into the lungs, throat and mouth. My companion, the Brother of Light, has explained to me that all things of the Spirit, all levels of the Spirit, have a counterpart in the plane of matter, the earth-plane. Thus my body (that body with its defective mechanism), represented the densest state of energy . . . earth energy. The water of the pond into which I floundered corresponded to the next phase of Spirit . . . astral energy. I recall quite vividly how this astral and psychic level of consciousness swamped the consciousness of the earth level, so that I seemed to float in a sea of colours and currents, and through shoals of strange shadowy floating creatures that bore no resemblance to fish, yet possessed faces. I remember that I was in a state of excitement, because suddenly and inexplicably, I could correlate seeing and experience together and *make sense!* The barrier in my mind (or rather in my human brain) was shattered. I could feel, and think and *know.* This was the first stage of death, though I was unaware of it as such. Even had I been aware of that transition, this new freedom of consciousness would have represented *Life*, not death to me.

'My Brother has instructed me concerning those Astral Worlds through which I passed. He insists that, although this may not be a part of the death drama for others, yet for me, it was entirely necessary, for when I had attained sufficient spiritual progress I would be joining the Band of Light Brothers, whose work is to release souls held fast in the illusions of the Astral Plane (as is the maid I knew, now the old woman in your cottage).

'I want you to understand that, when in incarnation, my soul knew the aridity of a mind, imperfect and imprisoned. In its passing to the next phase it needed to experience captivity in the emotional, astral plane of consciousness and to remember its feeling of freedom in the transition.

'This I now understand, so that I can comprehend with thought and feeling and compassion my sister (the maid's) state, caught as she is in these seas of delusion. With the help of that high consciousness to which my Brother of Light has attained, we will finally be able to draw her from illusion to Reality.'

*   *   *

For some days after this visit, my life was caught up in the activities of everyday living. I had little time to give to these affairs of the Spirit. One has to live a balanced life, especially when engaged in affairs not of this plane, and the Christmas and after-Christmas celebrations were normal, pleasant and relaxing. Often I give thanks that I am blessed by receiving a sufficient pension from my late husband to enable me to devote time to this spiritual work; time for inspiration and contact with other planes of thought, with no feeling of being constrained to earn my living. This is indeed a boon, for which I am most grateful. Balance is a vital factor in this work. One should appreciate the beauties of the earth-plane, together with the pleasures of contacts and communications with one's fellows here, as well as in the Hereafter. For a healthy life there must be balance in all things. I recall that Frances Banks had a great partiality for pretty clothes, especially hats, yet I have met nobody so close to the Spirit as she was, and so dedicated to 'my Father's Work'. She will ever be an example to me, and to those who knew her.

Thus it was almost the end of January before I was ready for any communications beyond that of the everyday reasoning mind. I recall that it was at the beginning of a cold spell, when next I was 'tuned in', quite unexpectedly, to the Voice of the Spirit. This time the contact and the contents of the communication were of such spiritual intensity that I was lifted beyond earth-consciousness into an awareness of a Divine Pattern such as I had never visualised.

I had had a busy day, an afternoon appointment and had settled after supper before my inglenook fire to read. The book was interesting, I was comfortable and I was absorbed, when, without warning, I experienced a change. I became sensitively aware of a difference in the radiation in the room. I can only describe this as a lifting of the whole feeling of the atmosphere. Something or Someone had entered that room and altered it. There was now registered within me a vital intensity, a flood of such Love that I was held in a deep meditation.

The book was put aside. I closed my eyes, and became still, responding with an inner joy to this consciousness. I waited, aware that a Presence filled the room.

Soon I knew. It was the Brother of Light, who had accompanied the Boy but had taken no part in his communications to me before. Now I knew that he was alone. I could not see him with my physical sight, as I had sometimes seen the old lady in the cottage. I could only sense his presence and build up in my mind's eye what, to me, was his appearance. I 'saw' him as a humble monk, for he had assumed the brown cassock and the waist-cord of a young Franciscan friar. I remember that the thought flashed into my mind . . . he *was* a monk once when on earth, and so he can re-clothe himself by thought in that habit if he so wishes. Frances had shown that this was possible in her *Testimony of Light*; and those who have the inward Eye well developed had often so described her as in her nun's habit, when she was 'with' me as I spoke on a platform.

These thoughts had hardly fixed themselves in my mind when words and sentences flashed into my brain, and I became aware that 'telepathically' I was receiving thoughts from my visitor. Hastily I caught up pen and exercise book, and I concentrated all my attention.

The Brother of Light sent his thoughts to me; as a telepathic sensitive I registered them, and I wrote them down. Here they are:

'My visit has a deep purpose,' I wrote from the telepathic communications, 'so deliberately I have chosen to show myself in the habit I once wore in an earth-life, and the "clothing" which I assume for work in the Shadow Lands. Indeed, I have "thought" myself here to contact you from some of the outlying suburbs (as I could call them) of these very regions of darkness. These are sad places, heavy with astral gloom, inhabited by the souls still resentful, still bitter about the fate they feel has overwhelmed them. These regions, however, of which I will now speak, are not in darkest hells. For the souls posited here can be easily released from the illusion of ideas of "death", *if they wish!* So often', and here I experienced a wave of sadness, 'they cling to the pattern of thought and feeling which they had built into their minds during their sojourn on earth. Thus they exist still in these "mind-forms", hating, rebelling, resenting, and wallowing in self-pity. Poor souls, they have scarcely moved from the limitations of the physical body!

'Our duty and service is to aid them to progress from the half-light of these drab abodes into the light and beauty of the higher planes of the Astral World. To do this we employ all possible means of changing their thought patterns, of dissolving fear and hatred by hope and love.

'Those faithful ones on your plane of life who send forth prayer, blessing, healing and love to these imprisoned souls know not the power of the great work that they do. For their prayers come like waves of sunshine to pierce the fog of despondency, to sweep away, momentarily, the drabness of half-light. Often, some soul is touched, some closely-held hatred is dissolved and some poor half-blind entity "sees" for the first time and is filled with remorse and healed by love.

'In other cases, we who work in these regions have perforce

to search for "instruments" or "channels", i.e. earth-minds which have the ability to contact and communicate with Us. Thus I contact you. From Brothers on the higher Planes of Learning, we were informed of your work in receiving and recording a *Testimony of Light*, which has helped many of its readers to prepare themselves for those other Planes of living, after the physical death and withdrawal of the soul from limitation. We observed you, we touched our thoughts with yours during your times of meditation. We became satisfied that we had discovered a useful channel. We wished to work with you.

'For this reason, your inner sight was opened to the presence of the old woman who still believes that she lives in the cottage which you now inhabit. Later, the Boy, who loved the servant and is working to "awaken" her, was enabled to contact your mind. For his initial visit to you, I "accompanied" him and a link was formed by which later work could be accomplished. You became cognisant of me; sensitively, you were able to "tune in" to the radiation with which I surrounded you. By such stages of expansion have you progressed towards the fulfilment of your task.

'From your cottage "lodger" you had learned the story of the Boy and his mother. He, an advanced soul in a stage of initiation which is incomprehensible to you; she, a young soul, inexperienced and stumbling in its progress. To your mind was imparted the joy of the fulfilment of one and the tragedy of the failure of another. Failure, I repeat, which has been brought over to this next stage of life. I refer, of course to the mother, whose bitterness has held her chained to the drab Shadow Lands, a soul refusing Light and Love, blinding herself to any opportunity of evolving, hating her present state yet rejecting the idea of any responsibility for it. She too must be awakened, my Friend; hers is a soul that loved beauty, yet loved it selfishly. Love itself for others, or even from others, cannot, it seems, reach her. Self, in its lowest, most limiting form, still imprisons her. She has no spiritual understanding, no belief and little hope. Neither her son, nor I, can penetrate through the black despair of her mind. If, as mankind has pictured for so long, there is a state of hell, then this must be it. Yet no soul remains in hell for eternity. God is Love. Love forgives, Love dissolves hatred. Love progresses into Light and Beauty. Love is the Law. Here we have an example of the lost sheep, for which the Shepherd returns again and again, to retrieve it from its wanderings. This is evolution; this is progress; and this is the Law of the Creator of all life.

'For this reason, your co-operation is needed. We can now bring her to you. You, who live in the material world, and thus are cognisant of its allures, its dangers, its tragedies, can act also as a go-between in the service of rescue of this poor benighted creature. Your mind, inspired by us, might reach hers and implant the certainty of greater Beauty before her, when she sees her mistake and is purged of her bitterness. This service could prepare her for the shock of her shut-in anger, of what she considered was the unfairness of the fate dealt out to her, partly by the fact of her child being "retarded" and partly by her own inability to redeem her self-centredness by loving.

'This is a Service We offer you. But it can only be accomplished with your willing assent and co-operation. . . .'

The words ceased flowing into my brain. I stopped writing. I sat, almost numbed with this new sense of responsibility. So far, I had been glad to help the old woman. I had been touched by the affection and constancy of the Boy. I had been uplifted spiritually by the shining Brother of Light. But this was a turn in the course of events so strange as to be almost bizarre.

Yet I had asked for Service. Slowly, it was borne in upon me that the choice had already been made. For some years I had petitioned in my prayers that I might 'fulfil that task which I had come to do'. The book *Testimony of Light* had been a direct answer and, I had felt, a fulfilment. Here was a further commitment. A great sense of wonder and awe filled me, as well as instinctive fear. Could I do this thing, carry out this charge? It seemed an almost insurmountable task.

I laid aside the pad and pen. The implication of all that had

46

been communicated to me was so overwhelming that I knew I could take no more at this session. There was then no further contact. My truly heavenly visitor had withdrawn his attention for the time being. I must await future happenings and be prepared for new turns in this most amazing astral drama!

I sat on in silence. No sentences of prayer, no petitions arose in my mind. I was simply and inexplicably 'tuned in' to another consciousness. Doubts and fears dissolved in me. Slowly, I realised some small comprehension of the perfect Divine Plan of progression for every soul. I became filled with awe and wonder at the realisation of the Compassion which is an integral part of a Creator whose Laws are immutable, yet compliant with personal freedom and choice. How little any of us here on earth can know! How infinitesimal is our range of conception of such Love. How petty and puny are our angers and our hatreds. How ridiculously short, yet how infinitely important is this little earthlife in the long progress of the soul!

Time must have slipped past without my cognisance, for when a friend telephoned me, I was astonished to find that the hour was eight-thirty and not, as I had thought, seven-fifteen.

After this, there was a lull, an entire cessation of contact with my other-world visitors. I put away my notebooks. For almost two weeks nothing happened. My energies were concentrated on different and more mundane tasks. Perhaps the communication from the Brother of Light had been too potent; perhaps I was terrified at the thought of contacting the autocratic and resentful Mistress. I know that I felt entirely inadequate. I know that inwardly I doubted myself. I even doubted the contacts. Could I, by any stretch of imagination, I asked myself, have made this all up? How could I have known about this tragic household? They must have dwelt in the neighbourhood at least eighty years ago. I had read nothing of the history of this part of England; I had never been interested in ancient houses, or in old families. Yet had I not 'seen' the old servant, who was earthbound, and lived in the thought-form of this cottage as it had been at the end of the nineteenth century?

Had I not held 'converse' with her mind? Had she not acquainted me with the facts of the Boy's life and death? Had she not given me a complete picture of her life in the suggestion that the freedom and relaxation and peace of this cottage were heaven indeed to her? So much a haven of rest indeed, that her soul negated the possibility of any other consciousness, even that of an orthodox idea of heaven?

The days passed, the evenings slipped peacefully by and I was no longer conscious of other things, either astral or spiritual, though at times I seemed to get snatches of a one-sided conversation. But I did not *want* to 'receive', and the thoughts faded from my brain. I was very much on the earth-level of consciousness. Perhaps that is where I ought to stay, I recall telling myself one evening, as deliberately I switched on the television.

Then the impression deepened that if it had all been make-believe as I told myself, then I would be troubled no more by these 'inner voices'. I, too, could live on the outer fringe of life, as most others did, and maybe enjoy it.

How far, how very far, had I moved from the uplifted awareness of Divine Love which had followed the communications (if communications they were!) from the Brother of Light!

I was to learn very soon what service was required of me; and indeed, to know that 'There are more things in Heaven and earth', than we, in our limited understanding, can credit.

CHAPTER SIX

The Mistress

The day, a Sunday, was bitterly cold. I sat by the fire in my snug little cottage, watching television. When that palled, I read the paper. But I was restless in my physical behaviour. 'Something' was about to happen, I knew, but it was mid-evening before I could even contemplate what this might be. Perhaps I could write, I thought; maybe ideas would come for a talk to be given later. I got out notebook and pen, settled myself . . . and then all ideas, all inspiration, all reception died. I was completely blank.

Irritated, I tried to unravel the Sunday Crossword, but soon gave that up. I opened a novel about Japan which, before I slept on the previous night, had enthralled me and began to read. The words were meaningless. I could not read; I could not write; the television programmes did not attract me. I began to feel that, in some strange way, I had strayed into a No-man's Land; I was lost in a region of mist, scared to go forward, terrified of retreating to whence I had come, and yet burnt up inwardly with an agonising fear that I could not stay where I was. This state of mind was so paralysing that for some time I sat without reading, moving, or even thinking. Suddenly I reached out and my fingers closed over my pen. Then I knew that I would have to write. But what? Still pondering this, I grew calmer, until that inward feeling registered that there were 'others' in the room.

Others?

I could not 'see' anything or anybody, not even my little old woman. I could only feel, with every one of my 'extra' senses stretched to awareness, that I was not alone. And it was not a happy feeling!

Whoever, or whatever, was present was as confused and fearful as I had been all evening. It also was as antagonistic towards me as I already felt towards it. Now, at last, I asked for help. I prayed, but what words I used, or what appeals I made to the Great Spirit, I do not know.

I waited. Presently came the flooding through me of the Light which I had previously experienced. My consciousness registered the thought form of the young Franciscan friar with the face of an angel, from whom I had received instruction earlier. This was the Brother of Light. I relaxed. Then I realised that he was not alone. In my inner mind, suddenly, I saw *her*. She was handsome, and apparently elegantly clothed in a dress of stiff black silk, which fitted tightly about her small waist and bosom, and flared out in a wide skirt to the ground. My visitor was quite a small woman, as modern women are measured, but she held herself well, her dark, neatly coiffed head held high, and her back fir-pole straight. Her presence imparted authority and arrogance. She moved with grace and dignity, but I noted that her full lips were drawn down at the corners in open contempt. Then I 'saw' the long silver chain and the locket!

So *this* was the Mistress. This was the entity corrupted by her own selfishness, her deeply-held resentment, who, by her mental attitude, was keeping herself a prisoner in those dingy suburbs of the Shadow Lands between darkness and Light. Here was the poor soul, shut away from the beauty she loved, yet lacking the cleansing of repentance that would free her soul for progress. Here was the charge that the Brother of Light had laid upon me. How could I carry out his instructions? *He* was One with her in Love; *I* was already shrinking from the restlessness of her presence.

Into my mind flashed words, and I knew that this woman's thoughts were already telepathic to me. She was standing gazing about the room. 'This is little better than where I have been,' she was summarising my home, 'only a workman's cottage.' Her lips curled in scorn.

At this I protested, sending out with some emotion, the contradiction to her statement. 'No, it is modernised, cleaned, and charming.' I looked about the oak-beamed room with pleasure and pride.

She made a gesture of dissent. So she must have received my thoughts, I decided. But had she as yet 'seen' me?

I tried to send more thoughts to her. 'It is light here . . . light and warm and pleasant,' I insisted.

She took no notice. Then she began to move about the room. She appeared to be examining the furniture and my pictures, with some interest. Was she seeing my pretty room as it now looked? Or was she still only conscious of the poor dark place which had once been the home of her servant? I could not know.

'This is better than where you have been,' I persisted, a trifle lamely, for I was conscious of her scorn.

She stopped for a moment, as if listening. She even looked in my direction. Then she turned away. I felt she had dismissed me. I was either a phantasy to her, or classed in her mind with one of her neighbours in her present place of abode. The idea was rather galling. I felt unsettled, and began to doubt that I could help her. Then I found myself dismissing her from my mind. Let the poor soul get accustomed to these surroundings; after all it was only her initial visit. I closed my eyes, and summoned all my strength to resist the unpleasantness of her presence. Slowly a change came; I was not asleep, nor in any kind of trance. But I became very still. My mind seemed to be reaching out . . . out. . . .

Presently this concentration was relaxed. I now became conscious not of the unhappy spirit exuding venom into my peaceful home, but of the presence of the Brother. He had not left. His thought was still with me. I began to register this. Then, as my hand reached automatically for pen and notebook, I realised that reception by telepathy was already beginning.

'So you are in doubt as to your acceptance of the task as

intermediary?' came the first thought. This was the Brother of Light, the advanced Being who was all-compassion, who in his wisdom saw this soul not as she now was but as she would become. I felt ashamed of my rejection. I waited. He went on very simply, and with a quiet Power that penetrated beyond my resistance.

'It is very natural . . . I believe that at this stage, some further explanation is due to you, and I will endeavour so to reach your understanding that we may become united and harmonious in this Act of Mercy.' There was a pause. A part of my brain registered the fact that the Mistress still prowled restlessly about my sitting room, but now it did not seem to matter. I had become impervious to the disruption of her presence.

The Brother began to explain the situation. His thoughts came clearly to me, and I wrote swiftly.

'I am known as a Way-Shower,' he flashed to my mind. 'Though I dwell in the Regions of Light and learn there and sometimes teach newcomers there, part of the service which I am honoured to perform is to take thought journeys into the Shadows and into the half-way regions, and from thence conduct any entities ready to set out upon the Way, after repentance and reparation, towards the Planes of Light. There is, as you may understand, a constant stream of souls passing upwards. Some have graduated even from the lower hells, some have realised their state and by constant effort have changed their thought patterns, have made reparation for their mistakes and so have gone forward into Light. Some remain stubborn and unrepentant and refuse our aid. In this category we must place your present visitor. You have already felt her unsettling presence and recoiled from it. How much more would you recoil, my Friend, at the *abode* from which I have brought her by thought!

'The Boy, whom you have now met in your inner mind, and whose life span on your earthly plane was short, restricted and extremely difficult, is a progressed soul. He has already graduated to the Plane of Learning, and he offered himself to me for service. Thus he accompanies me on some occasions to the lower Worlds. He is not yet allowed to proceed there alone, for there are many dangers which he could encounter, without sufficient knowledge, experience, and power to meet them safely. On one such visit he found her, who had been his earth mother. He was devastated at her plight, for although she had been cruel to him and he had been half-afraid of her, he had ever held a kind of dumb affection for her. There had been a strong soul-link between the two, forged in other soul experiences, a link which had, alas, not been harmonious. It was essential that this disharmony should be dissolved by love, but it was not accomplished in the relationship on the earth of son and mother.

'When the Boy passed from your plane and was awakened in the heaven World, he learned of the failure and was sad. He tried to send radiations of love to her to help her later years, but he could not reach her. Then she, too, left her physical body. His one aim now was to find her, and for that purpose he brought all his compassion to aid him. But he was not successful, because she had brought over with her into her new Life the same resentment and bitterness and selfishness with which she had faced the death-call. The barrier between them seemed insurmountable. Then, on our visit, he found her. But she did not recognise the progressed Boy. He was far removed from the pathetic retarded youth who had drowned in the water of the pond in their house grounds. She repudiated him.

'The Boy, her son, filled with love and compassion and with a great desire to help her to progress from her uncongenial abode, set his case before the Council of Wise Ones here. The records were searched. A clue was discovered in the soul pattern of the simple, undeveloped woman who had been his mother's maid and who had loved the Boy. The servant had also left her physical body, but had remained unaware of this change. She was not unhappy, as her Mistress, neither had she found herself in the suburbs of hell. She had clung in thought to her old form, and to her material abode, your present cottage. She was what you would call earthbound.

'The pattern began to link together. A Plan was conceived by the Wise Ones, and the Word went out for an "intermediary". Thus were *you* drafted to the cottage, unaware of the Pattern and Plan to be worked out. You will understand the rest . . . your consciousness of the maid and the appearance of the Boy, as well as the charge we have laid upon you to help in the rescue of the Boy's mother. May you fulfil this. May you, by your gift of inner sight and hearing, serve as the link for the release and progress not only of the ignorant earth-bound woman's soul, but also for this soul in its own tragic purgatory.

'You and I, my Friend, will act together as "Mind and Soul Channels". Realise that I am at hand to help you in any difficulties. Try to conquer your instinctive personality-reaction to this tormented but unrepentant soul. Presently, she will "see" you and a mind-contact will be made. I trust you will accomplish the mission for which your soul has asked and that the minor reactions of your personality will be superseded by the reality of soul-love.'

There was a deep silence. Then into my mind came the words, almost as a prayer: 'May the Light of the Christ accomplish this Pattern of Love through us.'

I was stunned. I sat on, every mundane thought in my mind silenced by the tremendous upsurge of spiritual strength which this great Being exuded. He was so gentle and wise and yet he spoke with such authority. After a while he faded into the background and again I became conscious of the elegantly attired woman who prowled about my sitting room.

There was an interruption by the ringing of the telephone bell and when I returned to my seat by the fire, the room felt strangely empty. The beautiful Presence of Light had gone and the restless unsatisfied soul had been returned to the dingy abode in the suburbs of the Shadow Worlds.

I put away my notebooks.

For two days following nothing happened. My energies were concentrated on different tasks. I was not conscious of this other World which is so close in thought and feeling to ours.

Yet at times I sensed snatches of a one-sided monologue, but when I tried to 'receive', the thoughts made no coherence and the words faded from my mind. I stayed very much on the earth-level and went about my daily tasks.

But on the third evening, as I switched off after the television news, I felt my senses stretch out like taut elastic, and I became 'tuned in' to the restlessness of my elegant visitor. She was prowling about the room exactly as she had been when the contact had been snapped some two days previously.

I experienced some surprise and a sense of trepidation. She had somehow managed the transition without the aid of the Boy or of the Brother of Light. How had she done this? Was she already remorseful and ready to co-operate? And in such a short period of time?

Then it was borne in upon me that there is no time as we here on earth measure hours and days. *Time is not* on the spiritual planes. *All is now*. After I had digested this, I sat back to contact, if possible, my visitor, trusting that she might be more amenable. I felt determined to keep this on *my* level, and not on hers.

'Welcome, bless you!' I sent out mentally.

There was no response. I might not have been in the room. She passed so close to me once that I felt sure she must have some awareness of my presence. Yet she gave no sign.

However, she was thinking, and my mind linked up with hers, so that I was reiterating her thoughts. I caught up my notebook and pen and waited. Her thoughts were neither pleasant nor constructive. She had not changed one iota.

'At least I am out of that dreary place,' ran the musings of the Mistress. 'Though this is not much better. Why is everything so dim?' (I had full electric lighting in the room!) 'I suppose this is another dream. A dream? The last was a nightmare. But there is something different. Could I be . . . am I really dead? Is there a continuation of life? If so, why is it so depressing? What about heaven . . . and hell? Hell?' She seemed to be considering this. 'Is there a hell? I never did believe in angels and harps, and I must admit I have not met any devils. Or have I? That horrible place I am in . . . are those there devils? No,' she shook away this thought. 'Then what are they? And where am I? D' I I really die? I can remember that heart attack. I recall yelling for my pills, but nothing happened. Then the pain, it did get worse, didn't it? What happened after that? Did I die? What happened to me? Why cannot I find my home? And why am I having to stay in this filthy slum? Wasn't my life unhappy enough? Shouldn't death be different?

'Life.' She paced the room, careless now of where she was, wrapped in a fog of self-pity. 'What joy did I ever have out of life? Money? Yes. Good looks? Yes. But was that enough? What happiness was there in my marriage to an old man? And what joy from an idiot son, a blow-fly of a creature out of lust with a farm-hand! I hated the child and he was terrified of me. An awkward lout with an inane grin. God, I deserved better, surely. It was a relief when he fell into the pond. Yes, I was glad when he drowned, my idiot son. As glad as when I was released and freed by the death of my elderly husband, before he went completely senile. I don't think I could have stood that.'

Here I felt that I could take no more. My peace of mind had evaporated. I was irritated, disturbed. I dropped my pen, and went out to the kitchen and prepared my supper. Tonight, I decided, I would simply listen if I had to, and nothing more.

To say that I was disturbed is an understatement, until I remembered the promise of the Brother of Light. Silently, I sent forth a plea for help. 'This is more difficult than I had expected.' Such evil and bitterness seemed to fill my peaceful cottage. Then I found myself whispering a prayer I had once read. 'Be with me, Lord, The night is dark; the Way not shown.' Later, when my fear had diminished, I tried to think of the woman's soul and to send thoughts of Love to dissolve its darkness.

It was some minutes before I could return to my sitting room with any measure of calmness. By then all was quiet.

My visitor was gone and the depression lifted. I put away my pen and paper. I knew I could write no more that night. Indeed, so great was my aversion that I wondered whether my pen would ever again record, or my mind 'receive' again.

And this was indeed so !

For it was nearly two weeks before I had any inclination to write, or felt any urge from a spiritual or astral source. I was worried because of the 'material' that was being poured into me for this book. It was to be a book; that I knew by now. I was certain, too, that the 'story' was already being enacted on the Inner Planes. It had been all right with the old woman lodger, and the Boy and of course with the inspiration of the Brother. But towards these later visitations I experienced a wholly adverse state. I felt rather as an actor must feel, pushed un-willingly into a play he did not like and into a scene which was abhorrent to him. After all, I was a kind of actor in this. I was interpreting the various roles. Again, I found myself criticising the whole of these unearthly happenings. I was very loth to be drawn again into an astral drama that now was threatening my own peace of mind.

Until one evening during the dark weeks of the coal strike. Sunday had been a 'lost' day. With millions of others, I had been cold all day, for the black-out on electricity (my only source of heat) had interrupted any intentions of writing or reading.

But by evening, our rota of black-out was over and I was again settled down to read, when I became aware of my visitor. She had again brought resentment with her and I recall shiver-ing slightly with anxiety. There she was in her stiff black dress, her small, proud head unbowed, her shoulders squared in a gesture of defiance, her long chain swinging, and she was staring at me. The Mistress had 'seen' me, or (should I write) had become conscious of me in her mind.

She began to address me, and yet of course, she did not speak as when in a physical body. She 'thought' her words to me, and her sentiments were not at all polite.

'You live here ?' she demanded. 'In a pigsty like this ?'

'It is not a pigsty,' I tried to make my thought as positive as hers. 'This is a home, an attractive cottage, renewed, rebuilt, and brought up to date.'

She glared at me. 'Date? My maid lived here after I . . .' she hesitated. 'After I. . . .'

'*Died?*' I broke in ruthlessly.

Her head jerked back. She did not contradict.

'You died,' I pursued. 'You became unconscious.'

She seized on this. 'Yes. Yes. I was unconscious. I couldn't see. I couldn't hear . . . I. . . .'

'You died,' I repeated, coldly determined to draw her.

I could feel the intensity of her recoil. 'Dead? I'm not dead. How could I be? I'm the same as ever.'

'And you live in your lovely home?' I persisted.

She swung round, avoiding facing me to give herself time to recover from this shock.

'My home,' she seemed to be trying to remember. 'It was a lovely house and a beautiful garden. But I've lost it. I can't find my way back there now. I have to stay in a horrible place, a hovel even worse than my servants would live in. I hate it. I hate the people too. They're mean. Why should I be made to stay there? Why? Why?'

She stood facing me as I sat writing. Evidently no question of my right to be in the cottage, or of her ability to contact me, appeared to disturb her feelings of venom towards everyone.

'You could be dead.' I felt I had to be brutal to get across to her.

'But I'm not,' she contradicted.

'What happened after you . . . became unconscious?'

'How should I know that? I told you, I couldn't see. Then I woke up in . . . a hovel. How can I be dead? I'm very much alive. I don't even feel ill any more.' She paused to consider this. 'I know. I'm asleep and dreaming. That is it. This is a dream, a nightmare.'

'*You are not dreaming.*' I made my thought as potent as possible.

She caught me up quickly. 'All right. I'm not dreaming. Then where am I?'

'Very close to the earth. I'm not dead. I'm still on the earth.'

The last phase of my thought did not seem to register. But she seized on the idea of being in some new place.

'Close to the earth? But I wasn't . . . before. Was I?' Now I could feel some dawning recognition of her state. 'I was in that terrible place. I was . . . I was. . . .'

She became a statue, fixed and frozen by fear. A shock must have torpedoed all former ideas, all hatreds, all vague hopes. I sat still, waiting. Poor soul, this was to be the moment of truth for her.

At last, she appeared to shudder at the awfulness of her interpretation. 'I was . . . *in hell*. Hell! That is hell! Oh, my God!'

Poor tormented creature. Perhaps I could reach her with a few crumbs of comfort. 'You were not in hell. Only in the suburbs of hell! Hell is far worse than that, I understand.' I told her, more gentle in my thoughts than before.

For a few moments she did not seem to comprehend.

'Suburbs of hell, you tell me? And hell itself is worse? Could anything be worse? Tell me that. Anything? Anywhere?'

'It could! It is!' I responded.

'Worse than that dirty hovel? Than those dreadful people?' I could see that her consciousness had fastened on this. She repeated the thought over and over. I realised that we had reached an impasse. Perhaps that would be all for this visit. I devoutly hoped it would.

But I was not prepared for her next outburst, or for the sudden gust of emotion that swept her.

'Suburbs of hell!' she exploded, and I prepared myself for what was coming. 'Why should I be there? What have I ever done? What did I ever do to deserve this? Did I steal or murder or oppress the poor? I went to Church on Sundays regularly. I gave money to charities. I put up with the dreary vicar for lunch once a month. I always paid my dues, I. . . .'

Suddenly I was aware of the Brother of Light. He stood away

from the Mistress and the Light of his presence radiated out over the end of the room. He made a sign to me, and then, quite distinctly, radiated thoughts to me, so that I found myself almost automatically repeating them in my own words.

'And hated your son? And bullied your maids? And despised your husband? And had no love in you? And no grace in your heart?'

The Mistress was completely nonplussed.

'But . . . but that was my own business! My own personal affairs.' She could have been stammering, had there been any sound to her thoughts.

Again, the Brother's words were echoed through my mind. 'And you think that . . . personal business hurt nobody?'

Anger flared in her. 'It hurt me.'

Again came the Brother's words. 'More than you realise. That is why you are amongst others who hated and hurt.'

'Amongst others?' The reference had found its mark. 'You mean those creatures in the . . . suburbs?'

At this the Brother was silent. I, too, tried not to formulate any thoughts. After what seemed a long, tense period, our visitor beat the air. 'But I did nothing, nothing!' Her radiations were so strong, she could have been screaming at me. 'To be near hell just for that! Just for that!'

The whole cottage echoed her resentment. I felt depressed and sad. Then I caught a ray of comfort from the Brother. Perhaps something could be done for this poor creature. I sincerely hoped so. One cannot be impervious to suffering. I felt that I could do very little. I could scarcely touch her. Yet was there not a great Being of Light, a Way-Shower, who was endeavouring to arouse some spark of remorse in this poor benighted soul?

I sat on for some time. The room felt empty and chilly. The Mistress, with her anger and bitterness, had sunk back to her ugly surroundings. The Brother had withdrawn his contact. I was sobered by this last episode.

Was I really in contact with a soul almost in hell? Could this really be death . . . and after? Was this truly the fate of entities whose lives on earth had been filled with selfishness; personalities who had hated and despised and hurt others? It was a frightening thought. If only we knew, I kept thinking. If only we were aware of the consequences of such negative emotions and such cruel actions. Of what use were the sufferings of saints and teachers and wise men? How had religion failed to emphasise this Law? Had not the Christ sent forth this Law of Love? 'Love thy neighbour as thyself.' Did that not include a son and a husband and servants?

The next evening, I had another visitor. It was not the hard unrelenting entity, the Mistress. Neither was it the simple unawakened maid, who, later, filled my thoughts with the warmth of love and compassion. It was the Boy. I felt that he was straight and tall now, different indeed in his spiritual body from the earthly ungainly shuffling counterpart in which his fine soul had been imprisoned on earth. His countenance was clear-cut and beautiful. I thought of his mother. If only she could see her son now. His smile was very understanding, for he must have caught my wish.

'My mother does not realise yet. She is new to the Spirit,' he excused her.

I interrupted his thought. 'New? She must have been there nearly a hundred years.'

I seemed to sense his amusement. 'Time is not. Only in your state of consciousness does time have any meaning.'

'But to have wasted over eighty years!' I protested.

'She has no thought of years, nor will she have,' came his answer. 'Yet she now has awareness of her surroundings. She is appalled by the darkness and drabness, for my mother had, and still has, an appreciation of beauty in her soul. Her garden expressed that; it was full of colour and loveliness. She revealed her exquisite taste, too, in her dress; always she wore beautiful gowns. These were, I grant you, expressions of an ephemeral nature, but they sprang from a quality of the soul. Mother is not a lost soul, you know.' His expression was very gentle. 'She is but misguided, misdirected and still held prisoner in the narrow circumference of her thought patterns.

'But,' his thought continued, 'we have a clue to work upon in reaching her, a sliver of light in the dark fear of her mind. We may be able to appeal to the unconscious desire for beauty still alive within her.'

'How?' I wondered, recalling the hard shell of this woman. But the Boy had withdrawn his consciousness and I was left to puzzle how the Spirit would be able to resurrect anything harmonious in such a conflict of rebellion and resentment.

* * *

I was recovering from a short, sharp bout of 'flu. My sitting room was warm and cosy in the cold February afternoon and enveloped in such an aura of peace that I surrendered myself to it. There came that stillness which, to me, is synonymous with contact with the Spirit. To my mind, nothing *was* at that moment; only a great power of peace, a shining quietude, a voluntary relinquishment of thought, desire and motive. 'I was, I am, I ever shall be.' The words slipped into my consciousness. Surely I had experienced this in some other state of awareness? But although, later, I realised that this had happened to me during the writing of Frances Banks' scripts for *Testimony of Light*, I did not at the time grasp the fact.

Sufficient then that the cottage was filled with a radiance and that the absorption of that radiance was what my soul needed.

Presently I became aware of the Brother of Light. His robe shone with a dazzling whiteness; his hair was pure gold from the brilliance about his head; he was light and beauty and peace. No other words could explain it. As soon as I was aware of his Presence, a single word resounded in my brain.

Desirelessness.

I knew then the meaning of that stillness. The channel of my mind had received the perfect equilibrium of my Celestial Visitor.

'Desire will ever negate peace,' came his thought.

'But desire for goodness . . . for joy?' I demurred.

'Still desire . . . and of the self, the personality and of

illusion' was the answer. 'Perfect peace asks nothing, has no
longings, no fears, no clutching at illusion.'

(Clutching at illusion? A strange metaphor. Yet so apt.)

My visitor directed his thought to me. Now it was pregnant
with purpose; after a while I followed the import of his
message.

He was explaining to me that the Boy's Mother, now dwelling
in the fringes of the lower Astral worlds, or the worlds of desire,
was hating her surroundings, loathing and scorning her fellow
prisoners and wasting her spirit in longing for the comforts and
beauty of her earthly home with all the privileges that material
wealth could supply. This was but a selfish yearning after the
ephemeral luxuries which she had never appreciated when
she had possessed them. But it was still desire, not a true
assessment of her own position or of the results of her actions.
There was no change of heart, no softening of pride, no remorse.
Desire still held her on the lowest rungs of the ladder of
progress and bound her there with its chains. Until this longing
for earthly things was dissolved, she would be unable to face
herself, or to assess her failures and successes in the light of a
more spiritual understanding; thus she was holding herself back
from progressing towards that very beauty which was a quality
of her soul.

'There is free-will,' were his last words. 'No compulsion
to review one's actions, no interference, no punishment, except
as she attracts that which she has made her own to herself;
no time-limit to her sojourn in those worlds to which her state
of non-grace has brought her. Only is there Love, the Law of
the Creator. And this Love will conquer, my Friend.'

Into my mind came the remembrance of Frances Banks'
'Blue-prints' in her book, *Testimony of Light*, and the gentle
way those who feared to examine them were helped and
blessed and healed. This then was the explanation. Until the
Mistress was purged of her defiance, she would never be able
to face the records of her earth experiences. These examina-
tions were difficult enough, as Frances had explained, for
ordinary 'good' folk. How much more frightening for one

whose conscience was seared by their recollection. Was this defiance an indication of deep fear? She had been separated from all she had desired and possessed in the material worlds. Now she was stripped and naked. There was nothing to hide herself from herself. She was experiencing a kind of purgatory. A feeling of compassion grew in me and I knew, then, that despite my reluctance, I would finish this work, if I was able.

One Saturday evening a week or two later, I was mending stockings by my fireside. The radio was tuned into the programme 'These you have loved' and music was breathed forth into my cottage and filled the room with beauty and joy. Sitting there, entranced by the purity and resonance of famous voices and great orchestras, I became aware that I was not alone. In the armchair opposite, in which I was used to perceiving the demure figure of my old peasant woman, sat another visitor from another world.

The Mistress!

She was perfectly still; her attention seemed to be rivetted by the music which poured into the room, and utterly absorbed in the lovely voice of a world-famous singer. She can hear, I told myself! Yet it was quite obvious that she had no idea of the origin of the music, nor indeed, where she herself was. She did not see me, and if she recognised my cottage sitting room from her previous visit, she gave no sign. She could have been back in her own drawing room in the great house where she had lived out her life; or perhaps in some opera house or concert hall where once she had enjoyed such music. Her 'body' was in repose. She was still 'clothed' in the stiff, black-silk, wide-skirted dress in which her maid had remembered her and over her bosom hung the long silver chain with the pendant locket. Indeed, she was the handsome woman she must once have been. Only now the expression of her face was warm, moved by the harmony and beauty that filled the cottage. She looked 'alive', glowing, uplifted. For some minutes I watched her, wondering if I was truly seeing her, even in my mind's eye. She looked different, released in some way.

I wondered if we could communicate at mind level, and very soon her thoughts came into my brain.

'I am dreaming.' The thought was quite clear; it revealed a lucid understanding of her changed circumstances. 'It is wonderful! So wonderful! I am away at last from squalor and misery.' Here her mind was choked with emotion. I could *feel* her tears. In my heart I prayed for help and release for her.

As if she had received the prayer into her consciousness, her anguish broke into words. 'Oh God, don't let me go back there, ever. Let me stay in this beauty.'

(And she had once designated my cottage a pig-sty!)

Presently I became aware of her son, now a shining figure of Light. He stood beside her, yearning for recognition. Deliberately he took a position within any line of vision her 'sight' might have. The light of his illumined countenance flowed forward and encircled her, recalling her consciousness from absorption in the music. She sighed and moved. But she did not see him. Twice I felt him call her gently. 'Mother!'

She made no sign of having heard, nor was there any implication of recognition in her expression.

At that moment the programme ended. Music was silenced. The Saturday night play began. I did not move; this was too solemn a moment to interrupt. If only the Mistress could become aware of this loving soul who longed to release her. But she sat on, bemused, it seemed, by the dream she thought filled her. The play continued. Half-listening, I was not aware of the precise moment of the Boy's departure. Neither did I know when the Mistress faded from my inner sight. I only knew that before the end of the play, my cottage was empty of any visitors from higher or lower realms. I was left with a feeling of frustration. How impenetrable is the darkness of bitterness. How thick the shell of selfishness.

And what a sadness would be this poor soul's when she awoke from her 'dream'.

Sunday

My visitor came again tonight.

I had tuned the television into the B.B.C. 2 programme 'Music on 2' and composed myself to listen to the Hungarian pianist Andor Foldes and to enjoy the brilliance of his technique. Before the Schubert *Impromptus* were finished, I became aware of the Mistress. She was back in the chair opposite me, her whole being profoundly wrapped in the beauty of the music. Behind her was the Boy. He glanced across to me, and flashed me a message. 'My mother was an accomplished pianist. I loved to hear her play. But I was never allowed in the room, when she was at the piano. My presence disturbed her.'

I marvelled, for now, I thought, it is by your presence, your concern and your love that she is here, away from the hell of her hovel, the hell of her own making, to listen to music.

The Schubert *Impromptus* ended. There was a silence; then an announcement. Then the glorious music of the Beethoven *Sonata in C minor*, the *Pathetique*, filled the room. The Mistress sat, regally attired as in her earth life (for probably she could imagine no other clothing) and she was relaxed. She did not stir through the whole performance; she was utterly wrapt, and the expression on her face was profoundly moving.

There is beauty in her soul, I thought, poor thing! I felt myself begging her to change, to become responsive to the love of her unwanted son, to lift herself from darkness to Light through her own remorse. And all the while the Boy stood, watchful beside her, waiting with infinite patience for the power of his love to touch her and melt her hardness.

During most of the deeply moving sonata, she had sat with her eyes closed. In the moment of silence that followed its last notes she seemed to open her eyes and her attention was caught by something else. This was a pot of African violets given to me by a friend. It stood on the coffee table between us. The plant indeed was a thing of beauty, its pink velvety blossoms glowed in the muted light from a corner lamp. The Mistress gazed at it with obvious pleasure and I realised how much she must have loved flowers. Then I saw that she was puzzled; evidently she had not known such a plant in her life-time.

All through the Debussy *Preludes* she was immobile, listening to and looking at beauty as one starved from its lack, as she was, of course. The effect of this was moving. I could almost hear her saying to herself: 'Don't ever let me wake from this dream.'

The music ended. Before the introduction of the next programme my visitor had faded back into the shadows and the Boy was gone with her. But I felt that a preliminary step towards the release of a soul had been accomplished that evening, through a three-part sharing of the divine quality of Beauty.

Next day

In the evening, after the lamps were lit and the curtains drawn, I felt a great need for quiet meditation. I settled myself comfortably, relaxed, and began the technique which seems to suit my personality and my aspirations. After some time, as I was returning to every-day awareness, I saw that my little old woman was back. She was sitting in her usual place across from me, eyeing me in a puzzled and inquisitive manner. I was so relieved to contact her, for there had been a long gap since her last visit and she was much easier to work with than her Mistress, that I sent out a welcome.

'What she be doing?' I could almost hear the question, though of course there was no oral sound.

'I was meditating,' I flashed back.

'What's that?'

'Trying to be in touch with God and the Spirit,' I explained.

She appeared to make a gesture, shrugging away such nonsense.

'Praying? Never 'ad much time for Church-goin' myself. Or for God. He never did much for me.'

'He created you.'

She grinned. 'Reckon me father and mother did that.' Then she added, 'Only the gentry and the parson got time for such

67

as praying and hymn singing. Didn't do my Mistress much good.' (No, I agreed to myself, it didn't.) 'Leastways, I'm too old for that lark now. I don't 'ave to wait on 'er any more. I've got me cottage and victuals. It's enough for me. . . . It'll last me out.'

With deliberation I repeated, 'Last you out? What about the end . . . when you die?'

She was startled. 'Die? That's the end of you, eh?'

'I didn't say so. What about heaven or hell?'

'Don't believe in 'em. Being free and having my own cottage is all the heaven I want.'

So that was it. This was her heaven. No wonder she refuses to become conscious of anything else.

She sat solemnly watching me. 'You're a queer one. Thinkin' of death, and all that.'

'Don't you?'

'No, never. Coffins, and goin' under the ground. Ugh!'

'But we all have to die sometime.'

She was getting annoyed. 'You do keep on so about dying.'

'Do you believe that some part of you lives on?'

'There you go again,' with exasperation. 'No, I don't.'

'But suppose you do . . . live on after death,' I persisted.

Her little face closed up. 'I'll wait till it comes to it to find out.'

Trying to make my thought casual, I sent out, 'Perhaps you won't have to wait long.'

She stared at me, and I could feel anger rising in her. 'Well, that's a fine thing! Not long, eh? You'll be telling me I *am* dead, next!'

'Are you?'

'No, I ain't. If I were would I be sitting 'ere talking to you?'

This was a bit tricky. 'You might,' I thought, and she picked it up quickly. 'Yes, indeed, you well might.'

She was dumbfounded. 'Well, of all the. . . !' Indignation was choking her thought. After a bit she recollected herself. 'Excuse me, Madam, you must be ill. Shall I fetch you a doctor?'

'Yes,' I agreed, knowing that she was dropping into a trap. 'Do that.'

She sat cogitating a moment, and smoothing down her apron.

'Where . . . where will I get one?'

'You don't know a doctor round here?'

'I ain't seen one for years. I don't see folk much these days.' She hesitated, as if caught into some dim remembrance of other times.

'You don't really see anybody, do you?' I probed.

She seemed to stand up with a jerky movement, and drew herself to her full five feet of height. 'Why should I? I've got all I want.'

'All? Have you no friends, no acquaintances?'

'I don't want 'em,' with stubborn temper. 'I got me cottage.'

'Aren't you ever lonely?'

'No, I'm free. I don't have to work from morning to night for nobody, now.'

'Is that your idea of heaven?'

'Madam, *you* don't know what service is, you don't . . . domestic service.'

I agreed to that. 'But I know I wouldn't want to be alone in a world with nobody to love or care for. . . .'

Her face creased with surprise. 'Alone? I never thought of it.'

'Well, I suggest you think about it,' I flashed. 'And now will you find me that doctor?'

I could see that the difficulty of this was worrying her. 'I don't know where to go,' she admitted.

'Your Mistress . . .' I hinted.

' 'As been dead these ten years.'

'We're back to death again,' I prompted.

This time she really did look frightened.

'Yes, Madam, I'll fetch a doctor if I can.' At last she was not so sure of her present state. The first doubts had been thrust purposely by me into her mind. I closed my eyes and inwardly voiced a thankful prayer. When I looked for her again, I found that she was gone.

Next night

After an evening of letter writing, I decided on a half-hour of relaxation and meditation. All evening the cottage had held that deep *resonance* of peace, a silence that could be both heard and felt. There was a Presence, that I knew. But it was not until nearly eleven o'clock that I was sure a communication would be made. I took out my notebook and pen and waited. I was not surprised to find my mind almost immediately in contact with that of the Brother of Light. How strong was his thought and yet how clear and compassionate and wise.

He began without preamble. (I notice that the Higher Beings never waste words or thoughts. Their concepts are perfectly conceived and perfectly communicated.)

'We are aware of your exchange of ideas with the woman who was the maid and who is under the illusion that she still lives in the cottage which you inhabit. We sent thought into your mind, we put a deliberate challenge into the responses you made to her negative convictions concerning the Godhead, and the Pattern of human evolution. We watched the effects in the aura surrounding her astral body. So far the results are satisfactory. Your conversation with her has induced the first healthy signs of doubt concerning her present circumstances. Until this had happened, she was content to cling to her isolation within the dream of cottage life in which she has convinced herself she is living. At last, this concept is disturbed in her thought. She is beginning to wonder and to question the reason for the absence of her old associates.

'Not that she yet accepts any possible theory of death, or of inhabiting another world. That realisation must come slowly; and of her own accord must she awaken. Then she will be released. For now she is as one slumbering, and to her that is rest. But her soul waits to progress. We cannot force such an issue. She has free-will, and only when the soul is strong enough will her spiritual eyes be opened. She can remain, if she chooses, within her limited and stunted consciousness, or she can break through the illusions of personality that still bind her, to find Light and Love, and so be brought into conscious union with her soul.

'But she needs help and again your aid will be necessary for this collaboration. There will be other opportunities. We will bring her to you again and gradually her closed mind will be freed. We have devised a plan wherein she will see *for herself*, and grasp the implications of the change that has happened to her. Have faith and trust in us. We work only for her good, and for yours. We work also for the enlightenment of mankind, to dissolve the ignorance of illusion, the glamour of materialism and the separating selfishness of the temporal personality from the wholeness and oneness of the Spirit. This is part of the break-through of the Spirit for the coming of the new dispensation for the approaching Age. Be of good cheer. Peace be with you.'

April 26th

It had been a very long time since any communication had reached me, either from the Astral worlds of emotion, where the Mistress and her servant had become 'stuck', or from the Spiritual Worlds of the Boy and the Brother of Light. I had put away my notebooks and had been caught up in other interests, in lectures and groups and discussions with earthly friends, as well as in social activities. But this day, I was trimming off some withered leaves from a house plant and thinking actually of the menu I was planning for a little supper party on the following evening, when across my thoughts flashed the information, 'She's here.'

There was no need to enquire the implication of the 'She'. I knew. It was the Mistress. I felt that I ought to have known before, because of the warning of the feeling of restlessness in my mind. This, alas, was the signature tune of the Mistress. Her vibrations were, and still are, potent. In her earth life she was what we are pleased to call 'a character', a strong character, even a forceful character, but not a loving character, or even a lovable character. Death had not changed her at all; neither, it seemed, had her long unhappy sojourn in the Shadow Lands.

I seated myself, ready with pen and notebook. This time

there was no mitigating love from the presence or even the concentrated thought of the Boy, her son. Momentarily, I found myself wondering how she had managed to project herself in consciousness to my room, without the Boy's help. Maybe she had progressed; maybe she was 'seeing the Light.' Even as I thought that, I was aware that her mind had crossed with mine; but what was more exciting, that she could 'see' me.

With marked lucidity, the pattern of her thought filled my mind.

'I know this place. I have been here before.'

Now I knew that I could answer. 'That is right. You listened to music. Remember?'

She turned herself about and stared at me.

'I remember. Who are you?'

'I live here. This is my cottage home.'

'Well, I must admit,' grudgingly, 'it certainly is a better place than where I've been dwelling.'

'You don't like where you have been?'

She made a gesture of disgust. 'It is horrible! Mean, shabby, hateful. And the people there are evil, full of evil.'

'You've been in the Shadow Lands, or rather in the suburbs of the Shadow Lands,' I told her.

'Shadow Lands?' She considered this. 'You know about them? Have you been there, too?'

I flashed back a negative response. I could only hope that I never would see that place. I waited.

She wandered about, looking at my flowering plants, touching them with obvious enjoyment.

'It's all just a dream, a nightmare.' She had evidently picked up my thoughts about the Shadow Lands. 'It isn't *real*, you understand?'

'It may be a nightmare?' I was growing bold. 'But you're *living* in it. Why are you?'

She swung round. 'I'm supposed to be dead, didn't you know? At least that's what they tell me?'

'Who tells you?' How I hoped that in some miraculous way she had been in communion with her son.

'Oh, those hateful people there. They say we're all dead. I don't believe them.'

'But it's true.' This thought was projected through me. I couldn't have stopped it if I had tried. I knew now that a spiritual Force was prompting me. 'You did die. This *is* your next world!'

Almost wearily, she responded, 'You, too? You believe that? Are you, then, dead, too?'

'No. I'm still on earth.'

At this she was silent, obviously puzzled.

'But I can see you? You can see me? I don't understand.'

I waited, not sure how to answer this. In the church behind the cottage, ringers were practising on the bells. Their lovely tones surged about the room. I wondered whether her new senses were advanced enough for her to hear them. But she made no sign.

'That is because I am trying to help you,' I flashed as calmly and quietly as I could regulate my thoughts; 'help you to get away from the Shadow Lands that you hate.'

Immediately I could sense a change in her. Her whole 'body' seemed to respond with a new hope and joy that lightened her appearance. I could express this as a quiver of light passing over her.

'Oh, please, will you?' she urged. 'I will do anything you say. You see, I am very unhappy.'

Now we had arrived at the crux of the whole matter. I knew that this was my cue; I must not muff it.

'But you made many other people unhappy during your time on earth, did you not? Your husband, your maid . . . and your son.'

The light around her faded.

'My son was an idiot,' she snapped back at me. 'A retarded boy.'

'Your son is a fine and beautiful soul,' I corrected her.

'Is?' She caught me up swiftly. 'He died by drowning in the pond. Is he in this next world, too?'

'He is.'

73

'In the Shadow Lands? I have not met him there.'

'No,' I made my thought as positive as I dared. 'He is in the Spiritual Spheres.'

She contemplated this. I could sense her struggling with the preposterous notion of the existence of any other place than she had so far found in the next world. 'You mean,' a new note of hope seemed to resound about her, 'that there are places . . . different . . . from where I am?'

'In my Father's House are many mansions,' I quoted.

'Mansions?' The idea shook her. 'Mine is a hovel.' Presently the truth dawned upon her. 'Can it be possible? *Is* there heaven and hell then?'

'It appears that there is something like that.' I knew that this was a lame explanation, but now I could feel myself trembling. The 'atmosphere' was becoming tense, or I was.

Suddenly bottled up anger and bitterness rapped out from her.

'I suppose you are telling me that I am in hell! Hell? Yes, that could be the answer to my miseries. But why, I ask you why, should a half-witted boy be in heaven? And I, his mother, am condemned to what must be . . . hell? It's true, isn't it? I am in hell?'

'You . . . went to the place prepared for you.' I tried to make this as gentle as possible.

'I . . . I prepared this place?' She gazed at me, and hope seemed to die in her. Her face appeared to break up and to my inner sense apprehension it was as if she trembled, for her desperation of thought shook her whole being.

'Was I so bad?' This was the moment of truth; self-revelation and initial confrontation with the egoistic self.

'You had no love.' It was agony probing the soul of this pitiful creature. I did not like what I had to do, but it had to be done, and I was merely the Channel. (How different it had been with my old servant woman! There had been a 'give and take' in our tussle to awaken her; and there were already results which promised success. This contact with her Mistress had, at first, been irritating, and was now becoming heartbreaking.) I was but a go-between. The inspiration and impact were from a Higher Source. The answers I was to give were being imparted to me; and I saw that painful though this revelation must be, it was a purgatorial experience that was necessary to break down the hard shell of pride. Later, when she had been released from her self-prison, she would be amongst Healers (as Frances Banks had explained in her book). 'You had no love for anybody but yourself,' I flashed to her. 'You did not love your poor boy, nor your husband. Therefore you denied God. For God is Love.'

She seemed to have no thought, only an acceptance of her plight.

'But you loved Beauty,' came the words into my brain. 'And God is Beauty, too.'

She seized upon this hope. 'Beauty was everything to me.' There was sadness now in recollection. 'Music. Flowers. Lovely things. These were my life. The garden, the grounds about my house. I created utter beauty in them.'

'For others, less fortunate, to see?' The words were again prompted in me.

'No. My garden was mine. Private.' Truth was being exacted of her. I was silent, leaning back in my chair, with my eyes closed. There was no need to open them; I could 'see' with inner sight. Besides, I had to shut out the warm comfort and pleasure of my own tiny cottage. My throat became constricted, and I gulped back the emotion that filled me, as I was forced to watch this poor soul endure the Gethsemane of her failures. 'Please help!' I sent out a prayer.

A radiance seemed to fill the room. The Brother of Light, the Shining One, was projecting love, compassion, and healing sweetness from his consciousness to us.

The Mistress stirred. She, too, must be receiving this Light. A sudden idea penetrated her mind. 'Beauty?' she pondered. 'I was a pianist; an interpreter of music. Isn't that Beauty?'

'For yourself, or others?' How thorough was this Brother in his examination!

This time, she faced me squarely, and now there was a

glimmer of light about her. 'Mostly for myself, I suppose,' she admitted. 'But often I invited people to listen, too. There was a little old man, a neighbour of mine, a gentleman, but poor and lonely. He used to slip into my music room whenever I practised. I never minded him. He said my music made him happy. I was glad about that. Yes, it's true, I did want to *share* this beauty with my old neighbour.' For the first time there was gentleness about her.

I could almost *feel* the lift in the 'atmosphere' of the room. Here was hope. Here was the soul itself speaking, unafraid. Truly our Shining One was fulfilling his mission.

My visitor sat waiting. She seemed at peace at last.

'I am glad,' the words came to me, 'about the *sharing*.'

She relaxed into the first smile I had seen with her. Presently she sent a thought out to me. 'It is beautiful here! Can I stay?'

'You can come again,' was all the encouragement I could give. But she seemed to find this hope enough. She began to wander about the room. Now I supposed she could see it as it was, and not as the pigsty she had called it. She stayed a while beside my flowering house-plants. 'They are lovely. I don't think I knew this species.' Reverently she stooped and kissed the flowers. 'Oh God,' she breathed, 'let me go somewhere in this next world where there is beauty and sunshine . . . and music.' I felt sure that this was the first prayer that she had ever said, and really *meant*.

'Somewhere where Thou art.' The quotation came through me. The words were not in my thoughts. I was very aware of the Presence of this Light-Brother. I could only sit in silence before this great Being, in contemplation of the Spirit of Beauty in which he dwelt and which flowed out from him.

When, later, I remembered my visitor from the Shadow Lands, I found that she had gone. Back, I imagined, to her dingy surroundings; but now with a thread of hope lightening the darkness.

The transcending love of the great soul, whose mission it was to lift and guide such entities, lingered on in my tiny cottage.

Two days later

It had been a quiet day. I had not felt well and I had stayed by my fire, resting all the day. For although it was April and the sun shone brightly, there was a cold wind and April was as icy as February. By afternoon, a gentleness and tranquillity filled me. The atmosphere of the sitting room radiated that deep peace of the Spirit which I knew and loved.

After tea, I read through the 'interview' with the Mistress. My reasoning mind could scarcely credit it. Had it really taken place? These were uncharted waters indeed. Was I allowing myself to float out on some stream of imagination? Was I setting out to 'lands unknown'? I pondered the whole strange set of happenings, from the first 'sight' of the old woman in my cottage to her Mistress's visits and the contacts with the Boy and the Shining One. Was the veil between the Worlds really dissolving? Would this mind-communication between incarnate and discarnate become the reality of the future? This was heady stuff. I tried to rationalise all these events, but this led me nowhere. For if I decided that the entire 'story' was pure fantasy, then I must credit myself with an imagination range which I knew I did not possess. Besides, I had never tried to dream up the next act in this unusual astral drama. The 'current' scene always took my mind and my pen by surprise. Never was I prepared for what occurred after the initial scene-opening. True, I had been vouchsafed a vague outline of the mission that I was being called upon to assist. But a pre-glimpse of the next act I had never yet been properly and consciously allowed. If this was pure inspiration, then from whence did it arise? The deep unconscious? Were these archetypal figures, as C. J. Jung once claimed? How then account for the *life*, the vitality, in them? How explain the subtle, differing characteristics in each one?

Characteristics? The Mistress's personality was so clear-cut, so decisive; The Brother was enveloped in such a power of Love. How was it possible that I could be aware of their presence, before my mind had even registered any thought from them?

Then again, consider the 'conversations'. They were written

without a pause, and certainly with no time for me to marshal ideas and apt responses in my brain. Besides, I decided in my rational mind, would I have dared to have spoken as I did with the Mistress had I met her in earth-life? I knew I would not. She and I would have disliked one another intensely. There would have been an immovable barrier between us. Now she was in trouble and I had, perforce, to overcome my dislike and critical assessment of her, to find compassion for her state. Compassion? This brought me to the breadth and depth of the love which characterised the woman's unrecognised son, and to the infinite power of Divine Love radiating from the Brother. If these qualities were of the Spirit, then how infinite must be the Love of the Father Spirit of all, and how far beyond our comprehension!

Here, my reasoning mind came to a halt; it was out of its depth. I would rationalise no more. All I was certain about, then, was that I was indeed blessed that even a reflection of that Ray of Spirit should hallow my home and light my soul.

'This is a two-fold operation.' The words slipped into my consciousness, and I was instantly aware of the Shining One. 'But with many connecting links of emotion and many debts from past experiences to be settled. The maid who is earth-bound and the Mistress who languishes in the shadows were bound together by a love-hate relationship forged in other lives. Shall we describe this as "scar-tissue of their souls"? Scars on the physical body are the end-products of wounds in the flesh. So in souls, seared in past conflicts and never completely healed by love. Hence the "sickness", dimly remembered, which holds them back from the Light.

'Here, may I diverge and explain that the Council of Wise Souls, who directed this operation of release, purposely chose these particular examples from sterile lives to be reconstructed into 'events' and fashioned them into words which will be read by hundreds of minds of limited finite consciousness. We trust that it may, at least, serve to enlighten these, concerning the state of that which awaits them after physical death has severed body and mind. We pray also that, even with such a

glimmer of knowledge, they may begin the trek from materialistic concepts to discover that Centre of Divine Spirit, per-
vading all life. The Way lies inward, to the Light hidden deep
in the heart of man.'

Next day

At this point I was interrupted by a telephone call, and
afterwards, I could not regain the contact so as to continue
the script. So I gave up and went to bed, where I slept deeply
and woke up with tantalising memories of dreams. It was a
boisterous and wet day and with shopping chores over, I settled
to rest. A feeling of contentment filled me and I became joy-
ously aware of those with whom I held close communion in
the World of the Spirit. In late evening, an impression arose
in my mind that a communication was about to be made, and
I scarcely had time to find pen and paper, before the Brother
of Light was projecting thoughts into my brain.

'You are astonished, dear Friend,' he began, 'at some of the
ideas that have been flowing into your mind, concerning the
true explanation of the working out of the Pattern of Love.
Be not surprised. And doubt not the Divine Spirit and the
Plan. Widen the extent of thought. Cast from you the limitation of time. Thousands of years of earth pass as naught. Time
is not. It is but the attempt of incarnated souls to consolidate
what is only illusion. It is the limitation of consciousness
which accepts birth, death and separation as realities, whereas
they are but figments of blinded sight. When man's inner sight
is opened, time will lose its power and its urgency. Until that
new awareness of the flowering of the Spirit, destruction and
decay will remain accepted tenets of the inhabitants of the
earth planet; and error and disease will be the lot of man.

'It is these very errors of the separated personality which
have to be worked out to their ends and this may take hundreds, nay, thousands, of your light years. At the present stage
of progress (that is, the commencement of a further outpouring
of Light upon your planet, which coincides with what you
have termed a 'New Age', corresponding to the Age of

Aquarius), debts are being collected and responsibilities levelled which may have been incurred centuries before, even during the Taurean Age, or Age of the Bull, of Egyptian ascendancy. Before the advent of this advance in the spirit of man, his debts must be discharged, personally and nationally. Such advances are already indicated by the changes in social, industrial and national life; they are also foreshadowed by the discoveries in science, which are narrowing the dichotomy between matter and Energy (spirit). Patterns are being worked out, pieces fitted as in jig-saw puzzles, linking together lives, experiences, reconciliations, harmonies, into the pattern of evolution, according to the Divine Plan. Scarred souls are being healed from terrifying memories by the Light of Love and Wisdom.

'Thus, dear Friend, wonder not about the lapse of time (so-called) during which your maid and her Mistress have been prisoners in their own limited consciousness and bound by the separativeness of their negative emotions. In your light years this represents a period constituting over eighty years, the end of the last century to your current years. To them, it is but "an evening gone" in the words of a well-loved Christian hymn. The Band of Light here, whose duty and joy it is to aid evolution, are ever ready to re-enforce the power of Love even in the most humble circumstances. Thus they are co-operating with the Boy's love for his mother and for the servant. This release from the darkness of error is the final dissolution of soul-memories of tragedies caused by surrender to negative forces. Such sagas as this are being enacted in the Spiritual, Astral and material worlds without ceasing.

'Life progresses; evolution advances on all levels. The wider and more complete the spread of tolerance, understanding, forgiveness, the stronger and more potent will be the Rays of spiritual advancement which will enhance the evolution of man. The greater the spread of spiritual knowledge, the more speedy will be the enlightenment and upliftment of humans into harmony and peace.

'The Divine Energy of Life is One-ness, and every particle

of separated consciousness must be drawn back to the centre of all, the very light of creation, to God.'

*   *   *

In May and June I was extremely busy with material matters, with travelling and talks, and the notebook was put away in a drawer. There were no communications, mostly because I was not able to concentrate for long periods. I was not aware of any visitations. The work seemed to be completely held up. But whilst I was away on my holiday in July, I found myself wondering about the shining being who was called the Brother of Light. One morning after a period of meditation, the following thoughts seemed to be dropped into my mind and I wrote them down.

'We are but one company of those bands of Brothers who have attained some measure of light and wisdom. There are many such companies working in different spheres according to their classification, their progress, and their special lines of evolution. They vary in their interests and their duties; some are advanced in wisdom, some are proficient in science, some are great artists, some are skilled musicians; and there are Great Ones who work on the Healing Ray. But all are one in the law of service; service to each other; service to the great ones of higher proficiency; service to the less-developed souls, and service to the lost and struggling, but all dedicated in love and thought and activity to the perfect ideal of Divine Life. To such souls, balanced as it were on the ascending spirals of light, service without desire for recognition is the perfect motive. To them, the "white rose of service meekly worn" is greater tribute and honour than the human Order of the Garter to those Knights of the material world who wear it in recognition of valour.

'Our particular band is but an infinitesimal point in the Ray of Compassion, and we progress as our tasks find completion. For all is progress, whether in the sphere of matter on the earthplane, or in the dismal regions of the Shadow Lands, or in the peace of the Heaven Worlds, or in the intense activity and beauty of the further Spiritual Spheres, progress towards ultimate perfection.

'Through compassion one is enabled to sense the needs of one's fellows, and to extend a helping hand to draw them forward into radiant life. Our councils here sit in conclave, and tasks are allotted. Mine, as you already know, is to labour to release prisoners of illusion in this world, and guide them on their way to light.

'By presenting this "Astral Drama" to the earthplane, we hope that greater understanding of the Divine Law for all creatures will be engendered in the heart of mankind. Our purpose is to try to bring into manifestation the unity of life for all creation, for this is the working out of the Law.'

August 16th

That evening I was watering my tiny garden which is almost within the shadow of the village church, when out on the air rang the solemn deep notes of the church bells. It was practice night, and I had heard that young people came with enthusiasm to learn the technique of bell-ringing. I love the sound of bells, so, as I sprayed my petunias, I was wrapt and absorbed in the glorious peal of sound.

Thus, I was all the more surprised when I was suddenly aware of my little old woman, and 'heard' her words.

'Them bells are lovely! Haven't heard them for years.'

I went on with my task of watering. But now a new idea flashed across my mind and occupied my thoughts. *She can hear the bells!* Our earthbound woman can hear the bells, I told myself joyfully. Does that mean that at last she is awakening?

But it was not until later, when I was relaxing in the cottage, that I again became cognisant of the old woman. She seemed to be definitely tapping at my mind, so after a while I found myself laying aside the daily paper, and reaching for pen and note-book.

'The church-bells,' she began immediately. 'Years since they played like that. They used to, when the Mistress took herself to church, Sunday mornings. Then they stopped. Maybe there wasn't no-one to ring 'em.'

'You mean *you* didn't hear them?' I countered.

'I mean they didn't ring.'

'The bells have always been ringing,' I retorted, 'as they used to do. Perhaps you didn't hear them?'

She was quite put out at my stupidity. 'How could I *not* hear 'em, when I lives here close to the church?' she demanded irately.

This was a poser. I did not feel confident enough to confront her with the right answer to that, yet. So I changed my line of thought and started another subject.

'Did you find that doctor for me?' I asked.

'Doctor?' Her annoyance vanished. Confusion seemed to fill her mind. 'No, Madam, I couldn't find no doctor.'

'What! No doctors in this village?' I remonstrated, keeping my challenge on a fairly light level.

There was a pause. I could feel that she was struggling with this. 'Village?' She was stubbornly defending her position. 'Well, I ain't seen no doctors.'

'And no village?'

'Maybe I didn't look.'

'But where do you buy all your food?' I probed. 'There must be shops.'

She pondered this. Then with irritation, came the explanation, 'I gets all me own food.'

She wasn't easily caught out. I tried another tack. Her state of imprisonment in her own thought world had to be made clear to her somehow. 'And you like your neighbours?'

'Neighbours! I don't mix up much with neighbours. Just want to know your business. That's neighbours.'

'So you don't see them?'

'No, Ma'am. I told you I don't mix up with folks.'

She was obviously becoming fussed. I felt I had to press home my small advantage. 'Perhaps your neighbours are all dead?' I suggested.

Apprehension stirred in her. 'Dead? They can't be. I wouldn't be living 'ere alone, would I?'

'You do seem to have been pretty lonely, I feel.'

'I always kept meself to meself, so I'm not lonely,' she defended. After a few moment's thought, she brightened. 'But I know you, don't I?'

I had to be careful now. We were coming to the confrontation. 'Oh, but I'm different,' I said inwardly. She picked this up immediately.

'How . . . different?'

I had to choose my words. 'Well, you see, I'm alive.'

This floored her. 'So am I? . . . Aren't I?'

'Are you?'

Now she was really concerned. 'I must be! Didn't I 'ear the bells?'

'Only because I was there, too, my dear.'

'Only because. . . .' She dried up. Fear froze her thoughts.

Now I had to state it. Poor little soul, this awakening was not going to be simple for her. She had felt herself so secure for so long, and I was to smash it for her . . . all this illusion in which she had hidden for these long years. I must endeavour to keep my thoughts as calm and gentle as I could. I hoped sincerely that the Boy was somehow in touch with us, though I could not feel his thought. 'You see,' I began, thinking my way into this. 'I live here, too, and I can see the neighbours and the shops . . . and find a doctor.'

There was long silence, during which no thought passed between us. I kept very still, with my eyes shut, concentrating on the truth to free her soul.

Presently, questions seeped out from her. 'Why don't I? Tell me that. Why don't I see them?'

'Maybe because you are not living like once you did.' I knew this was a lame explanation, but in the stress of the occasion, and in the awareness of her rising fear, it was the best I could do.

A moment later, the vehemence of her reaction hit me. 'You're not tryin' to tell me I'm dead, are you? Dead? I'm alive! I'm talking to you, ain't I? 'Ow could I be dead? It's you,' she seemed to tremble, so that her image in my mind quivered, and became indistinct. 'I remember now. You kept talkin' about death before.' Now, terror enveloped her; she appeared to my inner sight to fade away into a mist. 'That's it! *You're dead!* You must be a ghost. Oh, Lord, I'm seeing a ghost! I'm seeing a ghost!' She was terrified.

'No, my dear,' I kept my thought as gentle as possible. 'It could be . . . the other way round.'

Immediately I knew that I was thinking to myself. There was no recipient of thoughts. I had lost the contact. The old servant was gone. She had fled from the frightening necessity of facing reality. I felt drained and tired.

August 18th

I had been listening to Beethoven's Fifth Symphony from the Albert Hall Prom. Concert and during it was conscious of the intense 'listening sound' in the room. I can put it no other way. I gathered pen and notebook and waited, for I knew that the Boy's thoughts were already materialising in my mind. It is strange how one knows the different vibrations of souls, yet is it so strange? In earth life, one can often tell, without looking round, who has entered a room. Why should this faculty be altered between the levels of awareness? I would be a very indifferent 'sensitive', if I should mistake my old fellow occupant of the cottage for the advanced soul who was her Mistress's son.

'Progress has been made,' came the Boy's communication. 'We are joyful. The dear soul has for so long closed herself into a thought world of her own which has no reality and no substance. This soul for much of her life on the earthplane was made to be submissive to others; thus she created a 'life' of freedom as her heaven, and refused to acknowledge the fact of death. Can she be blamed? Of course not. But it is for her to find reality. And slowly, she is drawing towards that boundary line between truth and delusion. She is slowly awakening?'

'But awakening to what?'

'She has no conception of survival after death, nor of a world of thought, though paradoxically she has created such a "world"; a cosy illusion of escaping from all bonds of service and with the earthly continuing satisfaction of eating, sleeping, arising.

'Now, at last, she is beginning to doubt that "world". This is healthy and it must be so. But as she comes to realise her aloneness, what will be the state of her poor untutored, closed-in-mind? Fear, of course, and terror for what comes next. Regret for the loss of her "projected heaven".

'And yet we wait in Love and Light to meet her.

'In earth life she was kind to me, and often protected me from the contemptuous attitude of my mother. Our old servant is not a "lost" soul as you once thought, only a strayed lamb, who has wandered into the tortuous thickets of her own mind which close her away from those Shepherds who would guide and succour her.

'Our task is to open her mind to the welcome that awaits her. As yet, she cannot see me, nor can she visualise the beloved Brother who pours the Light of Spirit over her. She can and will only concentrate on what she considers is the loss of her "freedom" and the collapse of her "world". But you, she can both see and be in communication with, as you have already proved. Already your thoughts transferred to her mind have set in motion a reversal of ideas. For at present she is certain that you are the one who has departed from earthly life; and yet she wonders. At least that is a start. When she "finds" you again in her consciousness, it will be your part to instruct her of the true state of her affairs.'

Here, the Boy broke off and I began to chide myself that I had allowed my willingness for service to put me in this most unenviable of positions. For how was I, who knew nothing of the experience of the next world, to convince someone who was already in it? The whole operation was palpably beyond me.

But the Boy had already read my thoughts.

'We are indeed asking much of you.' His thoughts penetrated like arrows into my mind. 'But, remember that you have the Open Ear, a gift of the Spirit; and that, from those to whom much is given, much is expected.'

Immediately, I felt rebuked, yet there was understanding and gentleness in all he communicated.

'You have free-will, of course, to cease the "sessions" with this imprisoned soul.'

But I knew that I had no choice. I had already accepted in my soul; only the personality rebelled. And already I felt a sense of kinship with the old woman who loved my cottage as I did.

'You are not working alone, dear Friend,' the Boy continued. 'We will always be near to guide your thoughts, to influence your choice of language. Always, we will pour the Light of understanding about you both as you converse, to mitigate her "fear of the unknown". Through us will pour the love and the power of the Christ for His "lost lamb"; but you must constitute the "channel" from us to her. You may be surprised at the way in which this will work itself out. But can you really doubt the outcome?'

I knew I could not. As the conviction established itself, a great wave of healing and peace and strength surged over me and my anxieties were relieved.

'There will come a point at which she will be enabled to "see" me in her own consciousness,' he went on. 'Yet not until some other measure of conviction has been applied. Be patient with her, and have faith in the Plan. Remember, Love overcomes all obstacles in the long run.'

Then his thought was withdrawn from me. Now I knew that I was truly committed, but I felt renewed trust and strength. I pondered for a while on how the actual advance would be made but, later, realising that I would have to 'wait and see', I switched off from my inner thoughts and turned on the television.

CHAPTER SEVEN

The Plan, Part I

One afternoon, late in August, I looked up from the book I was reading, and saw that I had a visitor. The old servant was back. Recalling that our last contact had left her terrified that she was seeing a ghost—me!—I wondered what line her communication would now take.

She was eyeing me with deep solemnity, and I wondered what she was thinking. I had not long to wait. Her thoughts flowed out to me. I reached for my notebook and prepared to listen and record.

'I'm not frightened any more'; telepathy now took over quite simply. 'If you're a ghost, you look *real* enough.'

'I'm not a ghost. I *am* real,' I contradicted gently.

'I expected you'd say that.' She was perfectly calm. 'I expect all ghosts do. But you ain't clankin' chains or nothin' like that, are you?'

'No,' I agreed. 'But then you see I don't come from hell.'

'Ooh!' This startled her, as I had meant it to do. 'You mean, there's *really* hell?'

'It isn't called that,' I amended, 'and it isn't like you might think either—I mean hell-fire and all that.' I hesitated, selecting my ideas carefully. 'Hell can be a Land of Shadows.'

'Land of Shadows? Why?'

'Because it is dark there. And dingy. The souls there live in shabby streets, in misery, with no love and no joy. They are unhappy people. They lived selfish and often cruel lives on earth. Or else they committed some crime against their fellows.'

'Crime?' She watched me, fascinated by what I was thinking, yet sobered enough to comprehend the meaning. 'What sort of crime?'

'Hateful actions that hurt others.'

'Like murder?'

I was surprised at her choice of wrong-doing.

'Yes, of course, murder, taking away another's life.' I hesitated. 'But murder is not the only crime. There is cruelty, lack of compassion, even towards one's own flesh and blood.'

'You mean your own children?'

'Of course. Even mothers have been unkind and unloving to their own children.'

Her thoughts seemed to explode. 'That's wot *she* did. My Mistress. She hated her boy. She was cruel to 'im. She didn't really care when he died, she didn't.' So the resentment was bubbling up. So the old servant harboured hatred, as well as a sneaking admiration for her former mistress. It was scarcely a moment before her thought touched mine again. Then she asked a question. 'Is *she* in the Shadows then?'

I asked for help in answering this correctly. The words were projected into my consciousness.

'Yes, I am told that your Mistress is in the Land of the Shadows.'

I could almost have described the change that filled her. The chuckle of satisfaction was as human as ever. 'She deserves to be! Cruel to 'im, she was, and hoity-toity to me. Mean, too. And suspicious of what I knew about her. Never give me as much as a "thank-you" for looking after the Boy, nor nothin' extra neither. Nor no days off. Oh, she was a beauty, she was! Treated us as slaves and 'im as a burden. So, if she ain't going to burn in 'ell as the parson used to tell us when I went to Sunday school, then she's getting herself lost in the Shadows, eh?'

'She has . . . poor soul!' I added.

'Poor soul? She, with all her airs and graces! She living in a dingy hole? Lost in the Shadows, eh? For ever?'

'No, not for ever.' I refuted this. 'Only until she has learned to be sorry for what she did. And until she forgives and learns to forgive others.'

I was astonished at the vehemence of the old servant's reaction.

'Forgive others. Her? What she got to forgive?'

'I wouldn't know that,' I admitted.

The old woman seemed to stiffen into a thin creature rather like a monkey, arms tightly folded over the breast of her astral body. She rocked herself to and fro in a sinister rhythmic energy.

'She's in the Shadow Lands,' she was talking to herself with relish. 'My Mistress is in the Shadows! In the Shadows, she is. I 'ope she stays there for ever.'

'That is not kind,' I expostulated, alarmed at the unexpected change in her.

'Kind?' Her arms sprang apart, and she drew herself up to her full five feet. 'So I should be kind to her, eh? I . . . after all she did to me? Kind to the likes of 'er?' She rocked herself to and fro, fuming.

'I'm told' (I knew that these thoughts were the projection of other minds than mine) 'that you will have to learn to forgive, too, or *you* might find yourself in the Shadows.'

This silenced her. She seated herself, stroked down her apron, and seemed to close herself away in sullen resentment.

'Talkin' to the dead,' were the thoughts that filled her mind. She had entirely forgotten me. 'Talkin' to the dead. T'ain't possible. I'm dreaming. That's wot. An' me in the Land of Shadows, with the Mistress? Oh, God, not that. I been so peaceful in me cottage. Why can't I stay as I am?' For a while she ruminated on this. '*She* says,' and I knew that she was referring to me. 'She says, she's real, not dead. She seems to know a lot though. And she's always talkin' about bein' dead. That's queer. I wish I knew what it was all about, I do. Who's dead? Oh, I know the Mistress is. I remember 'er goin' off in that heart attack. But who else? That's what I want to know. An' all this talk of forgiving. Why should I forgive 'er?'

She had wrapped herself up in her own 'thought-cocoon'. She was impervious to my thought pattern now. Presently, she faded back into her own illusory world and I was left thinking ruefully that my 'lodger' was going to be difficult to shift. Yet already she was questioning. But was that enough? Stubborn she is, I decided, and even malevolent. How would she act, I began to wonder and speculate, if ever... ?

Suddenly I knew. Well, at least, I consoled myself, my role of go-between is going to be exciting, if nothing else! With that thought, I thrust the whole problem aside, and went for a walk.

*   *   *

That autumn was a long period of pain and depression for me. The pain of an arthritic hip as well as emotional suffering from a personal sorrow prevented any possibilities in me of renewed sensitivity. It was an utterly sterile period; one of those dark moments in time when one is closed away from the phenomenon of heightened perception and entirely swamped by an absorption of suffering which is deeply rooted in the personality. This is something that comes to us all, whether we happen to be open to the contacts of a further world, a world of souls, or not. Perhaps this sterility, this despair, is more devastating in the artist, the mystic, or the sensitive, than in the man or woman who passes his life on the 'edge of himself', closed in behind the curtain of separation. It is well-known and recognised that such dark nights of the soul often precede a fruitful period of inspiration and activity. This might be explained because all suffering occurs through the personality and initiates that despair which arises from the erring acceptance of separation. It may be that the personality which clutches us back into the material life is already beginning to protest against that which the soul is trying to impart, that suffering only exists in the realm of the personality. The psyche or the soul itself is unmoved by despair and depression, because it inhabits a world where there is no pain. It may well be that these sorrows and tragedies are given us to enhance the true nature of the self, to open the way to closer contact with the soul, and to aid us in shaking ourselves free from the limiting hold of the transient personality.

For that heightened perception which is the joy of the artist, the inspiration of the genius and the manifestation of contact with higher worlds of the sensitive, is inherent in the soul which inhabits the realm of universal consciousness, and is nearer to the eternal One-ness of the Creator.

It can only arise, therefore, when the soul is less contaminated with the desires, fears and emotions associated with the lower self. To me, this widened perception is the joy of living; I am barren without it. I feel only half-alive, as indeed I am! So, at length, with the help of good friends and good counsel, I was enabled to climb out of this slough of despond. I began to think again of the work that had been laid upon me to do, and the parlous state of those poor entities still in the consciousness of fear and hatred and resentment that was persisting long after severance of mind and body. What had happened to them, during these sterile months? I had closed myself away because of my own experiences. I, too, had lived in my small self, enclosed in a web of suffering which had blurred my capacity for communication. Would these contacts ever return? I felt guilty, until I remembered that nothing could deter these souls from progress towards Light and freedom but their own selves. I also had to understand anew that all this was happening outside of time or place, and under the jurisdiction of Beings advanced in wisdom.

I therefore waited for renewed inspiration, and it came. I began to see that the journeys of these two prisoners had already been started, in our last contacts, and would no doubt have proceeded according to Plan. This encouraged me. Communication would occur when I was ready to respond.

And so it was. One evening in November, a strong urge filled me to play operatic records on my recently acquired record-player. The lovely voices of Joan Sutherland, Renata Tibaldi and others swelled out and filled the room with harmony. I sat silent, drinking in the beauty of the music, when across my concentration cut the vibration of a presence.

'She's here! The Mistress.' I spoke the words aloud, startled by the unexpected suddenness of her arrival. I closed my eyes, and allowed my inner sensitivity to register. Immediately, I was acutely aware of her. *She was dancing.* I could scarcely believe it and for some moments sat entranced at the change in the entity who had been so sunk in gloom in our last encounters. The Mistress was moving with utter grace to the rhythm of the dance tunes of *La Traviata*, her slender figure swaying with the lilt of the music; In her stiff silk gown she made a picture of elegance and charm. She 'looked' younger than when I had last been aware of her. I thought to myself, I suppose she can make herself look as she wishes to look, now that she is a spirit.

At this idea, my thoughts came to a sudden cessation. She *wants* to look young and attractive as once she must have done! She *wants* to dance and be happy. The Mistress is different. She has changed. What has happened? Immediately, I was keyed up and alert.

The music went on. The Mistress waltzed; she swayed; she bowed. She was entirely unconscious, I was sure, of me or of her surroundings. The consciousness of a new vibration in her assailed me. This was not the complaining, resentful visitor of the last call. I felt that she was released. She was experiencing joy for the first time since she had crossed the river of death. This was thrilling and exciting; I hoped that some contact would be established between us.

At last my L.P. record came to its end, and shut itself off automatically. I did not move. I stayed with my eyes closed and my inner senses waiting to pick up impressions. What will happen now, I asked myself?

I had not long to wait. The Mistress stopped dancing, but remained poised and uplifted in her new happiness. She seemed utterly absorbed in this unaccustomed world of rapture; she looked quite beautiful. Slowly, as though she was sighing because the moment had passed, she let her arms droop and her head bow. Then she straightened and began to look about her, this time with a more discerning and interested gaze than when she had visited my 'poor hovel' previously.

'How lovely that was! How beautiful!' I caught her thought

quite clearly. 'To hear music again. To be back. . . .' Her mind
was suddenly stilled. More soberly, it resumed. 'But I'm not
back home!' She began to walk about the room. 'I'm here
again.'

'You're in my cottage home,' I prompted, anxious that she
should communicate with me.

'Your cottage home?' So I had reached her. 'Who are you?'

'Oh, just a friend! You came to see me before. Don't you
remember? You said I lived in a pigsty.'

She swung round. 'Did I say that? I couldn't have been
seeing it. I'm sorry. It was unforgivable of me to say such a
thing. Your home is pretty . . . charming!'

The Mistress apologising! A miracle must have happened.

'Thank you,' I flashed out to her and she smiled, as the
thought contacted her. 'I'm glad you have come.'

'So am I!' was her swift response. 'To be released from that
awful place. You see, I've been allowed to come here again.'

'To come here?' I echoed her thought.

She confirmed this with a distinct nodding of her head, and
a charming smile. 'Yes. To listen to your music. You see,'
wistfully, 'I loved music so much, when. . . .' She seemed to
catch back the thought of her material life.

'When you were on earth?'

She nodded agreement. 'Yes. I wish I'd known then all that
I know now.'

'Why?' I interrupted her.

'I suppose because I would have lived differently. I mean
I would have been kinder. How was I to know that I would go
to such a terrible place, be amongst such horrible people, live
in such sordid surroundings? I've suffered,' she could scarcely
control her emotions. 'But now, I've been allowed to come here
again. *They* said that was just a beginning.'

'They?' I echoed.

She seemed surprised that I did not know about Them.

'They are Helpers and Teachers,' she volunteered. 'And
They are kind. For a long time, I thought they were Church
visitors and I could not see what they had to do with me. We

used to have Church visitors for the poor; and I never thought of myself as *poor*. At least not until I learned that I was to stay in that hovel, that it was my home. I was told that I was "poor in spirit."

'That shook her,' was my impulsive thought, and was immediately startled when she came back at me. I had forgotten that this telepathy was a 'two-way contact'.

'I was shaken to my very depths,' she went on. 'And I could not lightly get over such implications. Also, it was said by a sweet-faced woman, one I had seen visiting before and who had impressed me as being happy and charming and sincere. She was so different from the creatures who lived in similar hovels to mine. I thought about this very deeply and when she came again I went forward to speak with her.' She paused. 'I cannot remember quite what we talked about, only that I begged to leave my dark abode. I think I told her about the music I had heard here and about your flowers. She seemed to understand. Then she said I could come again if. . . .'

'If what?' I prompted.

'If I stopped resenting where I was. I do remember telling her that there was only ugliness there; one could not help resenting ugliness. She agreed about that, and asked me if I loved beauty. I told her about my garden, my greenhouses and all the lovely plants that once I had; and about my music. She understood at once. She said that she would help me to come here again to hear the music if I would accept my present place.'

'And you have?'

Now she was wandering about the room. She stopped before a cyclamen plant, and fondled its white blossoms with a gentleness that was surprising in such a hard and arrogant personality.

She did not turn to me as her thought flashed the answer.

'I am trying,' she admitted, and then, ruefully, 'It is not easy! They are not my type of people. At least I thought they were not. But now, I have to remember that I, too, am poor in spirit.'

For the first time, pity and compassion for this suffering soul overcame me. It was a tragedy indeed, that, with all the advantages she had been given in her sojourn on this plane, she had failed to listen to the teachings of the church she had patronised as lady of the village. 'Love one another' and 'Love thy neighbour as thyself'. She had not even loved her son.

She stayed for some time, but she did not communicate with me again. She seemed happy just to be in my cottage. I put another record on the gramophone, and she sat entranced listening to it. Then she slipped away, but this time she left a warmth and an aura of pleasure which I would never before have associated with the Mistress. She was, indeed, changing.

Three days later

The day was cold and wintry. After lunch, I ensconced myself by the electric fire and tuned into the B.B.C. Third Programme. A concert was in progress; a performance of Tchaikovsky's Fifth Symphony was being given. Relaxing in the warmth and peace, I gave myself up to the beauty of the melodies and after a while seemed to slip into another world.

She is here, came the startling information, the Mistress; only this time it was a pleasant recognition. My inner senses stretched. Yes, there she was, sitting in one of the room's armchairs, utterly wrapt in the glorious music that filled the cottage. I watched her; she appeared calm and content.

When the symphony finally came to its tremendous close, I flashed a thought to her. 'Welcome! Nice to have you back!'

She withdrew herself from her world of harmony. 'It was magnificent!' and I knew that she meant the music. How her soul must have starved for it! 'Thank you for allowing me to come into your home. I love being here!'

Thanks from the Mistress! And her first use of the word 'Love'! I was overwhelmed.

For some minutes she remained relaxed, peaceful, unthinking. I switched off the radio, for I knew that sooner or later she would communicate, and I prepared pen and notebook. Presently I caught her thoughts. They appeared to me to drift quietly into my mind, so different from her first explosive contacts.

'I know now why I am in that place of half-shadows,' she began, a little diffidently. '*They* told me.'

'They?' Again, I echoed her word, prompting more information.

'Yes. The sweet-faced sister came again. She brought with her a wonderful spirit, a man with the face of an angel. His eyes were so beautiful, so blue, as if Light was shining behind them. I do not know who he was, or from where he came. I had not seen him before and I am sure I would have noticed that face if he had visited us. His whole figure *shone*. Even to my dark hovel he brought light. It was the first real ray of light that I had seen, since . . . since. . . .'

'Since you had died to the earth-world and had come to life in the real world?' I prompted.

She acquiesced. 'That is correct . . . if you can call it life! But I have now been informed that this was all the life which I had prepared for myself. This was such a completely new idea . . . it still is.' She broke off, musing within herself. Then, 'It was the angel-man who told me that! At first, I was overcome by him and a sort of power that was about him. I suppose he has great authority. I felt timid.' The Mistress timid? I marvelled. 'You see, he was so different from the horrible creatures who inhabit my present world, and yet he had come there among them. And he spoke to me. He had a kind gentle voice, yet the words he said to me were terrible, frightening!' She hesitated. I could feel that she was battling with a wave of emotion, but this time it was neither anger nor resentment; it held all the tragedy of the knowledge of lost opportunity. 'I would never have believed such words, had they not come from one such as he. They were Truth. I knew they were Truth; that made them no less accusing. He said that I had *starved my soul*. He said that I had fed only the *emotions and desires of my personality*! Terrible, terrible words. What a denunciation! That *I* should ever have to hear such an accusation. Starved my soul? Fed my emotions? I could scarcely bear it, and yet,

97

and yet, I could not deny it. It was true! Suddenly I seemed to see through his eyes. I looked at myself. It was devastating.'

I waited, holding my mind still, for this was the time for silence. This was the moment of truth. I was awed and very moved.

'He said more, but I cannot recollect it. Then he went away. I felt as if I had been squeezed through the mangle that my kitchen maids used on their washing days. All hope had left me. I knew that I was in hell and terror-stricken by the thought that I would be there for ever. Do I mean terror-stricken? Perhaps not . . . it was all confusing. But the sister stayed with me. She must have stayed beside me through all my panic. I'm not sure about that, you see it was such a shock . . . those terrible words being true, I mean! Such an indication of failure and the cause of the punishment I had brought upon myself. I had never thought of myself like that. Perhaps I had never thought about myself at all, and I had never really believed about a life after death, only vaguely listening to sermons about heaven and hell. But now I knew! I *was* in hell, that was it. But was I to be there for ever?'

Her thoughts were flooded and closed away by emotion.

'Not for ever,' I murmured. 'Not for ever.'

She swung round to me. 'That is what the sister said! You believe that, too?' Her thoughts raced ahead, not waiting for an answer. '*She* said I wasn't really in hell, only in the precincts of what she called the Shadow Lands. I imagine that must be the real hell, a place that criminals and utterly wicked people make for themselves. I wasn't a criminal, or was I? I hated my child, but I never physically hurt him. Sister said I was not in the real hell, only near it! Near enough! Near enough! But she was very kind. She was certain that I need not stay there. You believe that? At first *I* couldn't (believe it, I mean), but she persuaded me. It was my first glimmer of hope after all my misery. I *felt* her compassion. It was too much. Not to have to remain in hell? I, who was always so proud, I wept.'

She sat silent for a long time. 'I was ashamed,' she admitted at last, 'ashamed of losing my control before her; humiliated because she knew all about me. Yet comforted by what she was saying. The love in her flowed about me; it was like sunshine. I think I fell asleep, yet, when I woke, she was still there; and I felt refreshed and quiet. I was strong enough then to listen to what she had to explain to me. It was almost like a mother talking to a child. I wonder whether if I had borne a normal child I could have loved him! She made me feel like that! She made me wish I had been kinder.'

I could hear traffic in the street outside. I was aware of rain beating against the windows, yet I was held within another world of consciousness. I was tense with the sharing of this poor soul's emotion. *I* was learning, too, as never before!

It seemed a long period of emptiness, before my visitor resumed.

'This was my first experience of kindness. The sister stayed with me. We talked together. She was gentle. I even wondered what she had been on earth. I was sure she had been a lady of circumstances; she had the air of good breeding. Strange that one carries over to this other Life, *what one was*! That was a point she made with me. It was difficult at first for me to understand. I was, she said, exactly *what I had been*. Because of my failures on earth, I was in this predicament. She even quoted the Bible at me. Once I would have been extremely angry at anyone taking such a liberty, but now was different. She was in authority, I had to listen. "As ye sow, so shall ye reap," she quoted. I looked at her calm face. "So I am reaping," I asked her, though I knew. Her answer was as I had expected. "You did not sow love or harmony; you withheld compassion from your son; you scorned your husband; you treated your maidservants harshly." I couldn't bear any more. "Stop!" I begged her. "Are you then an avenging angel?" She shook her head and smiled. "No. I am but like you . . . a pilgrim on the Way." She, a pilgrim on the Way? Then what was I? . . . a speck of dust?'

The Mistress bowed her head. She no longer wept, nor was

there any sign of resentment. Remorse in her was too deep for tears, too *real* for rebellion.

'I was seeing myself as I was,' her thoughts continued, 'and I was appalled. Appalled! I was stunned by the revelation. I knew then that this was the reason why I was to live amongst these revolting people, these hateful creatures, for I was like unto them! I was one of them. I, too, had sown as they must have sown.'

What was there for me to communicate? One was helpless in the face of such revelations. 'But the sister,' I prompted, 'she gave you hope?'

The response to this was startling. The Mistress sat up; she was like one casting away a burden. I found myself thinking of a branch of a tree, bowed under the weight of snow; and as the sun came out, the snow slipped away and the branch lifted and was free and straight. So she seemed.

'Oh, yes. She has given me more than hope. She asked me if I had ever loved anything. And, oh joy! I could answer her truly. I had the feeling that I was calling out, "Yes, yes, I did love. I loved beauty, I loved flowers and colour and music. Believe me, I did love, I still do. That is why this drab place is so terrible. . . ! Can I never see beauty again?" '

'And the sister?' I flashed the question again, for she seemed to have passed into a reverie.

She stirred. 'That lovely face *glowed*! Positively glowed! It seemed as though a light burst about the sister. And I shall never forget what she said. "God *is* Beauty. So you loved God, though you never knew. Dear Soul, thus you have His Passport. It will take you from here and darkness into Light and Beauty." I could have knelt at her feet. "But now," she charged me, "you must learn to love creatures, your fellows, your companions, your son." "My son? Is he here, too?" She shook her head and smiled. "You can help these souls. You can be kind and understanding with them." I knew then that it was going to be a grim lesson, but I must not fail. She asked me then if there was anything I would like to do to help me during this kind of probation. And I thought of you, and your flowers and your plants . . . and the music. I thought that if I came here sometimes, as I had already done, it would give me strength to succeed, it would be a kind of solace.'

I was profoundly moved. 'Bless you!' I sent out the new emotion in me, amazed at the change my own feeling for this soul had undergone. 'Come as often as you can!'

Her gratitude was pitiful. 'Thank you! I do sincerely thank you!' Hesitantly, she allowed her thought to venture forward. 'I have the happy feeling that this is my first step out of the Shadows, my very first step. I am grateful . . . deeply grateful.'

Before the impression she had created in me had dimmed, she was gone.

*   *   *

It was about fourteen days after the last entry that my little old woman returned, and this time *demanding* my attention!

I had had a busy morning, shopping, ironing, cooking; and as my arthritic hip was troublesome, and giving me much pain, I decided to rest with my feet up all the afternoon. I had, moreover, two most interesting library books which I had only recently borrowed, and I much looked forward to reading them after lunch. I made coffee, and was washing up after my meal when my super-conscious' mind became aware of the old retainer. This is odd, I thought to myself, she usually contacts me when I am sitting silently reading, or listening to the radio, or watching television, yet now she seems quite imperative to be 'heard'. As I washed dishes, I could distinctly feel her pushing herself into my consciousness. This was something new, especially as I might have frightened her on the last visit.

Then, suddenly, it was borne in upon me that she had something exciting to communicate. Clearly I became aware of an urgency, an excitement. But I will finish my chores first, I decided, then have a rest and glance through the new books. The old lady will have to wait. So I ensconced myself in my favourite chair near the window, relaxed, and started to read.

But I had reckoned without the determination of my visitor. Again and again, awareness of her mind intruded itself between the book and my concentration.

'I'm excited,' the signal seemed to be flashing. 'I've found out something!'

About three o'clock I became drowsy; I was re-reading sentences, and yet not getting the drift of the printed material. I put the book aside, deciding to take a nap, and closed my eyes.

No sooner had I done so than the 'communications' began to flow into my mind; they went on clearly and vividly for at least a half-hour. I was entirely unprepared, and would have to rummage in a drawer for notebook and pen, and this would interrupt the flow. This 'repartee' between my ghostly visitor and myself was so fast and so thrilling, and absorbed me so utterly that at the time I did not realise that I would have to try to recall it all later for the book. This was indeed daunting.

But I decided to write it up later. However, after tea there were telephone calls and chats. It was not until nearly seven o'clock that I could settle to the work, and then I was very conscious of the difficulties. For the spirit of the old lady had gone. After our talk (which, alas, I had not recorded), she had faded out. Now I must write from memory. This was no easy task. I sat down and began to write.

I recalled the air of excitement, and the old woman's intense desire to tell me her news. I recalled the shock of her first words.

'I know now,' she had begun, flinging her thoughts into my brain. 'I know wot it's all about! You remember our last talk? I thought you were dead, eh? It scared me. I can tell you it did! And I 'oped I'd never see you again. But I was wrong, Madam, I was wrong. One of us was dead, all right, only it weren't you! It's me . . . it's me! I'm dead, or wot you call dead, ain't I? Ain't I? I found out, you're on earth, like I used to be, and I am . . . well, I don't rightly know where I am, but I ain't livin', least, not like I used to be.'

Well, some progress has been made, I thought to myself, and tried to urge her on to more communication.

'So you've found that out,' I flashed back. 'How did you?'

She seemed to recollect for a while. 'It's like this,' she began to think at last. 'All your talkin' of a doctor, it was, Madam. "Get a doctor," you says. An' where can I get a doctor? I thinks. I ain't seen a doctor for ages. I worried about it, and then it brought me up to somethin' else. I ain't seen nobody else, either, for that matter, I says to myself. An' then I begins to worry. Why ain't I seen nobody? Why didn't I know where you could get a doctor? Where was I? I seemed to be always on me own, nobody ever come to see me. It must 'a been ages, an' yet it didn't seem long. I was still in me cottage, an' yet it weren't like me cottage, somehow. Then again, what was you doin' in the cottage? You seemed to be livin' there, but then so was I. An' I never used to 'ave any one, let alone a lodger.'

So I was a lodger, was I? Poor little confused soul, this was a painful discovery for her, this loss of the home she had so much loved and had clung to, imagining herself in a permanent heaven on earth. Her train of thought followed on, and it was not difficult to realise the mind struggle that she must have passed through.

'I sat and thought and thought about it, I did. I wondered if I'd gone barmy. An' I can tell you I felt bad. Doctors, I tells meself, when did I last see doctors? An' why? An' where? Madam, I felt I'd lost me memory altogether. Then, it all come back. It was after the Mistress died, a long time after. I got to know that much. . . .' She stopped.

'Yes. Yes. Go on,' I urged. 'What was your last memory of doctors?'

She was still and silent without thought for so long that I decided she must really be confused. What else could I do to help her? I sent out a call for help from Those who were watching and waiting.

Presently, the old servant's mind seemed, miraculously, to have cleared. 'My last memory?' she repeated slowly. 'You want me to say wot I remembered? Oh, Madam, it weren't 'appy-making, it weren't. It were a real shock. I cried about it, I did.' She paused, emotion choking her. I waited.

'It was in a 'ospital, Madam, in the infirmary. I fell down on the floor of me cottage . . . I well remember that now; but what 'appened after? I dunno, only I woke up in the infirmary. I knew it was that 'cos there were nurses and doctors. Yes, Madam, that's where I last saw a doctor. An' I couldn't bear it, 'cos I begun to know I must 'a died.'

'And if you did die,' I suggested, 'you're still "alive", aren't you? You can think and you still *are*. Was that all you found out?'

'No, Madam, not really all. I 'ad another shock, that was the one wot told me . . . I come back to see you 'ere.'

'But you *live* here,' I interrupted. 'Where had you been?'

She seemed to shake herself. 'That I don't really rightly know,' she admitted, a little shamefacedly. Then, controlling her feelings, she went on. 'But you weren't 'ere. I sat a long time puzzlin' me 'ead about it all. An' then . . . then I "saw" the stove weren't 'ere no more. My stove 'ad gone, so 'ad my furniture, my bits and pieces, all gone. The place 'ad changed, it weren't like my cottage no more. It was what the Mistress, drat 'er, used to call "elegant". It made me cry terrible. I'd lost my 'ome. I felt I'd got no place of my own. An' I didn't know where I was.'

I swallowed a lump in my throat. This was very real and very moving.

'An' . . . all of a sudden I knew like. I knew I was dead. There weren't no doubts about it. I'd died in that 'ospital. I'd died, God 'elp me, yet I wasn't buried. I 'adn't any grave that I knew of. An' you 'ad my cottage. You was alive. I was dead. I 'ad no right to be here. I was frightened. I went out, an' I wandered about.'

'You poor dear! You'll find a new home, you know. Someone will come to fetch you now.' I tried to cheer her.

The old woman shook her head. 'No, Miss, I'm lost. I got to find me grave, anyway.'

'You don't need your grave,' I flashed to her. 'That's where

your old body is. You've got a new body now. You're going to
live in some pleasant place.'

For the first time she looked straight at me, and the confusion
in her expression moved me strangely. What a sad thing is
ignorance, I thought. If only people *knew*. There were so many
without even religion; such numbers who lived purely material,
physical existences, without hope or knowledge of a future.
So much ignorance. Heaven or hell, or nothing. Such were the
beliefs. I mused sadly on this, forgetting my visitor. When I
recollected my thoughts and consciousness, I discovered that
the old woman had gone. But where? I could only send out a
prayer for guidance for her. At least, she was now awake.
What must follow?

*   *   *

It was several days later, and I had been away from my
cottage, and was now home. The hope had been with me that
I could finish the book before I entered hospital for a hip
operation. Now, I felt the hopelessness of this idea. There was
much more to do, I knew, and little time to do it. Perhaps it
was this thought that made me search out my manuscript and
read the last few sentences. It must have been this contact
of thought that brought the old woman back to the cottage; for
there she was, sitting opposite me, and smiling. It occurred to
me then that I had never seen her smile happily before. So
something had happened. I did not have to concentrate or
wait, for no sooner had I seated myself than she started to
'relay' to me in the most excited and confident way.

'Hello, Madam,' she greeted me. 'I been lookin' for you.
You weren't 'ere. But I found you, with lots of other people.
Yes, *I found you*. You see, I got to go on, soon, an' I wanted
to tell you what's 'appened to me. Yes, I did want you to
know.'

'It sounds as if something very exciting happened. Do tell
me,' I encouraged, and put aside the fact that I was tired and
would rather have gone to bed, or read an exciting book. I

brought out my exercise book and pen, and settled to record. Then her thoughts started, and so impelling and compelling were they that I had a real task to keep up with her. My pen simply flew over the pages; my mind was enthralled; concentration was complete. She seemed to have fastened herself into me so closely that when the script was finished and she had gone her way, I felt drained.

'Oh, it was excitin',' she began. 'After a bit. At first as I told you, I was scared. I felt I 'ad to look for my grave, as I told you. I started to wander about, an' I didn't know where I was, or which way to go. An' I kept sayin' to meself, I'm dead. But I must be goin' somewhere. I must be goin' somewhere. Where? I thought, I wish I could find a Bobby like in London. But there weren't no Bobbies, least I never saw none. An' I remembered wot you said. I'd got a new body. Only it didn't look no different. An' sometimes I thought about the Mistress in 'ell, but I didn't feel sorry for 'er. Only I got afraid I might be goin' there, too, and I'd 'ave to see 'er again. I knew I wasn't going to do wot she told me, this time, even in 'ell. I felt more sure of meself, like. An' you told me I would find a pleasant place, so I reckoned it wouldn't be 'ell, where she is! An' I walked and walked; then I started to call out loud: "Someone come and find me" . . . like you said . . . "Come an' find me. I'm here." Oh, it seemed a long walk all alone. An' then I *saw* 'im, a little old man sitting on the side of a hill. "Who are you?" I says. "I'm me," he says. "So am I," I says. "Only I'm dead." "So am I," he says. We weren't gettin' very far, were we? So I says, "I'm afraid. I only just found out I'm dead." "Oh, you needn't be afraid," he says. "Where are you goin' now?" I says I didn't know, maybe to 'Eaven or to 'ell. Then I asks him the way to one or other of 'em. 'E didn't rightly know about 'ell, he says; but it weren't that awful far to Heaven. Oh, I was cheered up at that, I was. I thought, "Per'aps he's a Bobby . . . a 'eavenly Bobby." An' d'you know, 'e seemed to read wot I was thinkin'. "No, I ain't a Bobby," he says. I was a bit depressed about that. "Well, 'ow do I get to Heaven?" I asks him. "Can you show me the way?" '

There was a pause, and she almost chuckled.

'You know, Madam, 'e give me such a queer answer. 'E made me go all embarrassed. "The Way," he says. "The Way? It's simple. You just says your prayers. That's all." "All?" I answers 'im, seein' all hopes of getting there gone. "I don't know no prayers, I don't." "Course you do," he says. "Your Mam taught you *Gentle Jesus*, an' *Our Father*." I didn't ask him how he knew that; suppose I never thought about it. Anyway, I cheered up a bit, 'cos I didn't 'ave to say anything fancy. *Our Father*, "Yes, I remember that."

'Only I wasn't really sure if I did. It had been a long while since I'd said it. 'E must have known that too about me, 'cos he says, quick-like, "Come on, then. Let's say that together. It'll maybe bring someone you know." An' I knelt down like I used to when I was little in Sunday school, an' we says it together. *Our Father, which art in Heaven. Hallowed be Thy Name.* . . . I was cryin' when we finished, cryin' fit to break me heart, an' I couldn't see proper because me eyes seemed all wet. Then I felt that the little old man was 'olding my hand, he was, an' I thought he would lead me the right way. I turns round to thank 'im, and to look at 'im, an' . . . an' he'd gone. An' there was my Dad, my old Dad just like 'e used to be. Oh, Madam, I stared at 'im, I did. I says "Dad? Oh, Dad, are you dead, too?" An' 'e laughed. My old Dad, 'e laughed. "I been dead a long time, my girl," he says. "So 'ave you. We been waitin' for you to wake up. We been waitin', your Mam an' me." '

I could feel the tears smarting in my eyes. But there was no time to wipe them. My visitor was rushing on, and I mustn't miss a single word.

'Waitin', they was, Madam. Waitin' for me. I cried and cried, it was so wonderful. My Mam and Dad. I couldn't 'ardly belive it. It was all so new, so different. Well, then my Dad 'e took my 'and, and we walked up that hill. But I couldn't walk. I was so tired. I tells my Dad I was too tired to walk to Heaven that time. An' 'e says to sit down a while an' rest. So I did, an' I must 'a gone to sleep. And I waked up in such a lovely place, an' there was my Mam and Dad. They looked so sort of 'appy . . . and young-like. But they said it wasn't really 'Eaven yet. It was so beautiful, I thought it must be.'

At last she paused. Her face was radiant. She was still in her servant's dress, only now she looked different, taller somehow and serene. I was so moved, I could only flash out to her my joy, and happiness. Bless you, I tried to say; you're on your way, you're on your way.

'Yes, Madam. Yes, Madam,' came her answering flash. 'It was you tellin' me about bein' dead an' death, an' about getting a doctor. That made me think. Oh, I'm so glad you did, now, an' I'm happy with my Mam an' my Dad, an' the others. That's why I asked if I could come back, just to say it's all right, it's all right. An' I'm sorry I thought your cottage was my cottage, because it ain't. Oh, Madam, I'm so glad I knows now I'm dead. It's all so different from wot I thought. I ain't afraid no more. I'm 'appy, Madam, I'm 'appy. An' thank you for helping me. Here's my Dad. Yes, I'm comin', Dad . . . I'm comin'.'

And she was gone. My little old woman was gone on her way. I wondered whether I would ever see her, or be aware of her again.

CHAPTER EIGHT

The Plan, Part II

But, of course, I knew inwardly that I *would* encounter my old 'lodger' again. The saga was not finished yet. This strange astral drama must work itself out to the climax of its appointed end. There was much to happen, much to be accomplished. Part I was finished; Part II already beginning. The Plan and the Pattern were being accurately followed. One soul had been released from ignorance and self-imposed separation into at least partial awareness; another soul had found a great Truth, that *God is Beauty*; and this Truth, as the sister in the Shadow regions had told her, was her Passport to Progress.

As I wrote these words, I became aware of the concentrated thoughts of the Boy, and I felt enclosed in the love that flowed from him. I relaxed, and presently the Presence of his advanced Brother of Light lifted the atmosphere of my cottage room into a harmony and peace that was like a still lake under a harvest moon. I sat in silence. The aura of light filled the cottage; the silence could almost be 'heard'.

Into my contemplation filtered the thoughts of the Brother. His mind reached out and touched my own. To me it resembled music echoing faintly through my very soul; a choir of angels could not have harmonised with more sweetness. Then, slowly, and without effort, words flowed into me. Through the Channel of this Light, I was receiving from the Spirit.

'Dear Friend,' came the telepathic communication, 'Our visitation is one of joy and thanksgiving. An entity has released itself from the enslaving chains of ignorance. The fog of illusion that had persisted from its deep immersion in the materialistic concept of an earth-plane life has been dispersed.

Now it has accepted severance of the surviving personality from the body-personality. Now it is ready to be led forward into Light, and into that conscious union with the soul which is the commencement of the Way of the Spirit. It is a lost sheep found; and for such there is rejoicing in the Spheres.

'But also a sad and closed-in personality has begun to apprehend the great lesson and truth of love. To this entity has been revealed, even if but the merest glimpse, something of the nature of the God-head. Beauty is love in action; and love is beauty fulfilled. Creative love is our Father, and by His Word brought He forth beauty. Thus, without true compassion and love, there is but ugliness; without the light of the Spirit there is but darkness. And without light there is no vision, and the soul languishes.

'Yet love never ceases, for it is poured forth eternally from the Creator, the Source; and light can never be completely extinguished for it is of the very nature and essence of life itself.

'Each soul, created by God, must return to God, since it is incarnated light seeking the eternal light, as a river seeks the sea. Is it not written that "In Him, there is no shadow"? Only shadows are cast by obstacles that close away the sun, by the belief in separation from the sun, by the illusory concept of division of Spirit and matter. Such shadows inflict pain and suffering even to despair. But redeem matter by the light of the Spirit, and the long evolution of man will have been achieved. This is the true interpretation of the Redemption, of which the supreme example was given in the ascension of the Christ.

'Yet because man has free will to make his own progress, he oft chooses shadow and separation, until slowly he learns by suffering. For ever there is light beyond his self-imposed darkness; and always there is love encircling his own self-immersed separation.

'And many indeed are the channels to light; and too numerous to count, the ways of the Spirit. For no individual is forsaken; no soul left to wither. Despair and suffering are but steps upon the Way, for all is evolving into light. The Father of all is love. His Spirit is light, and His creation is beauty.

'My Brothers and I will watch joyfully as beauty recreates love and love brings light into this awakening entity who in this last existence was chosen for the Boy's mother; and who, at length, is now emerging from a chrysalis of matter into the winged joy of a new birth.'

The message ended. I laid aside my pen. I could do no more that night. But love and beauty lingered in my cottage; and I had the impression that this was a blessing for the New Year which was upon us. If only this 'communion of love' could go out with this book, then the 'sharing' of love would be complete; yet if but a few who read, tune in to this Spirit, the light will have penetrated 'even in our darkness'.

*　　*　　*

A week or so before this last series of scripts, I was fortunate enough to attend and speak at a conference concerning Life after Death, held in an Anglican monastery. There was a fairly representative audience; some already convinced of the survival of the personality after the death of the body; some who had come with no previous knowledge or experience of the subject; and some orthodox and erudite persons who were ready to discuss (and some to argue) the pros and cons of such beliefs within the accepted tenets of the Christian faith. It was a lively and interested audience; amongst them were many nuns, and some Brothers from various Anglican orders; sweet-faced Sisters to many of whom this approach to the hereafter was completely new, but who were already open-minded enough to be seeking knowledge.

I mention this conference because I believe that it played a very real part in the working-out of the Plan to awaken and free the two entities known to me as 'the old woman in the cottage' and her Mistress. I also include a reference to it, because its effects seem to prove both the efficacy of prayer and the power of love, that self-less *giving* which alone is of the Spirit, in the divine work of healing, blessing, and enlightening.

One evening, during the conference, when the entire audience were gathered in the lecture room, the subject that was initiated by the chairman concerned specific experiences of 'communication with the dead'. He recalled and recounted many examples of extra-sensory perception wherein the so-called dead had communicated with him through famous sensitives, many of whom had now themselves passed on into another life. One example given was that of the spirit of his own father, who presented most conclusive evidence of his identity. Then a woman writer and sensitive who was present was asked to contribute her experiences; and all listened with great and absorbed interest.

Suddenly he called on me. I had not expected this, for my talk had already been given that morning. I was taken by surprise and was completely off my guard. Without realising what I was doing, I began to tell the story of this book. I spoke of the 'appearance' of the old woman who was my unseen lodger; I mentioned the Mistress who hated her son, and who was hated by the servant, the sad plight of them both and of what I felt was my task in aiding them and of writing about this astral drama. I could hear myself speaking about a subject which I would scarcely wish to broadcast before the writing was finished. But they were so interested that I imparted a great deal of what had happened up to that time. The words seemed to flow from me without restraint, as if I was intended to speak them.

And so I now believe I was!

For after the talk, many of the nuns came to me to say that they would pray for my 'visitors' in their own communities, so real already were these spirits to them. I was much moved. After the conference I received letters from others who had been present who would be sending forth their petitions for grace and light to be vouchsafed to them.

'More things are wrought by prayer than this world wots of,' is a well-known quotation. If I needed proof of that, I have it. For it was less than a week after I returned home to my cottage that the contact which I have already described in the last chapter was made. The old servant had 'awakened'. Though still confused, she had accepted the fact of the death of her body and the survival of her mind. She *still was*. She had escaped from the fog of ignorance and was following blindly along the path to light. Then, a few days later (in our time), she returned to impart her good news. The scales had finally fallen from her spirit eyes and she had seen and recognised her own father, who had been sent to guide her on her way. And this had been revealed only after she herself had repeated the long-forgotten prayer of her childhood, *Our Father, which art in Heaven.* . . .

The prayers and blessings of those dedicated women had been heard and answered! A soul went forward to a new life, and there was rejoicing in the 'courts of heaven'.

How truly does the Brother of Light speak of the power of love! How little we know of the influence for good that our prayers can bring both to the living and the so-called dead. I recall that this was stressed by Frances Banks (herself an ex-nun, who knew that of which she spoke) in the book *Testimony of Light*. Prayers and blessings and love, she suggested, are 'received' by our departed dear ones, and are to them as a 'staff upon the Way'.

But how much more wonderful is prayerful help to the sad 'earth-bound', the unrepentant, the loiterers and self-prisoners in the shadow precincts! Can we not remember this, and act upon it in love, as the religious showed us?

*   *   *

It was but two days after the last writing when I found myself carrying on, as if we had never left off, from the last visit of the Mistress. I had just switched on the television to hear the news before six, when I heard myself speaking aloud a conversation, and with my visitor from the Shadow Lands! So she had returned? I grabbed pen and book, and let the words flow through me. This was a new development, for at first I was not aware of a visitor. But I could 'hear' and answer the thoughts; and there was such urgency about them, that I could scarcely write fast enough to keep up. This was truly inspiration; at least, these thoughts had not been in my consciousness. Indeed, I had never envisioned the possibility of the situation that was now arising for the sojourner in the Shadows. This, to me, was an entirely new turn of events. I wrote almost under dictation, rather as the *Testimony of Light* scripts had been transcribed. I might have been intrigued if I had had time to pause and assess the gist of my transcription, but I had not. I wrote almost in a fever.

I had been writing for some time, recording what could have been an imaginary conversation, before my visitor herself 'appeared' in the room and I became conscious of her. So her thoughts must have travelled out to me. The Mistress was indeed progressing in adjustment if she was able to do this.

It all began with a fragment of conversation which was spoken aloud, I not realising what was being said. It was a provoking topic, indeed.

'There is re-union after death, I have discovered,' came the surprising opening to the discourse. 'Even here, in this dreary place, there have been meetings between friends, and relatives. Yes, I have witnessed them; perhaps this is because I am now taking more interest in my companions. They are not always happy or welcome re-unions, which is strange, until one recollects what manner of place this is. I was talking to Sister about this and I enquired if I should be brought face to face with some that I had known on earth. I shuddered a little when she admitted that this might happen. But she was so comforting; she always is! She told me that if I progressed in compassion and service towards my fellows here, I would move on towards the Light. I felt that maybe I would not have to meet such as I had disliked on earth.'

'Those you disliked?' I found myself thinking. 'Were there none you liked or loved?'

The Mistress must have received my thoughts for back came

her reply, without any preamble. 'No,' she said, 'None worth remembering.'

Greatly daring, I sent back the thought. 'But you had a son?'

'If you could call him a *son*!'

'He was your flesh and blood. Don't you want to see your son again?'

'No, I do not.'

My reaction to this must have startled her. 'I know *I would*!'

As I wrote, I felt a change in the room. She was here with me. So great, I concluded, had been the shock of this, that her urge to defend herself had precipitated her into my consciousness, and I had become aware of her.

She had seated herself in a chair opposite me. There was a pause, as I accustomed myself to her presence.

Then the words flashed out at me. 'I might, if he had been like any other boy.'

'What do you mean by that?' I enquired, though I knew.

There was a period of silence. Then she communicated again.

'My son was an idiot. He could not think clearly and scarcely could he speak two words intelligently.'

'Poor boy!' I sent forth the pity, yet as I did so, I could only think of the bright spirit of the advanced soul that she scorned. 'How terrible for him!'

This moved her. 'Terrible? For him? He knew nothing at all. The embarrassment was for his mother.'

I tried again. 'But your son must have died. Is that right?'

'Yes. The poor fool was drowned.'

'Then,' I volunteered, trying to draw her. 'Surely he will have changed. He can't still be unintelligent!'

'Changed? Why should he? We don't change after death. I have not changed, have I?'

'No, you have not changed.' I wanted to add 'unfortunately'. Her quick mind seized on this. '*Should* I have changed?'

'I do not know,' I sent back to her, and she looked relieved. 'But you did tell me about the Shining One and the sweet-faced Sister. They suggested that you must change yourself.'

She shrugged this away. 'Oh, that is different. They meant change my *ideas* about others; they told me to try to accept the creatures with whom I am now in contact. Yes, I am doing that; at least I hope I am.' She sat passive for a while; then she smiled. It was the first really natural expression of pleasure that I had seen with her, and it altered her appearance completely. The arrogance melted. 'I am trying to have more compassion. I think I am succeeding.'

'The Shining One will be happy,' I flashed to her, seeing a mental picture of that fine face. 'What makes you think you are succeeding?'

'Because I am still allowed to come here. This is a great privilege; a joy; a holiday. To me it is penetration into light, even if only a passing escape from gloom.'

I smiled to myself. She was learning, and fast. I watched her, praying that the gentler expression would remain. Then I sent forth a pertinent question. 'What do you imagine has happened to your boy? Do you believe he is shut up somewhere with other maladjusted boys?'

'You mean . . . other idiots?' The hardness had returned. The lips had folded into a tight line again.

'Yes, I suppose that is what I mean.'

She was without thought; the possibility of such a fate for her son left her blank, and without concern.

'What else could there be for him?'

Now it was my turn to be really shaken. 'But he has left his physical body. He is alive in his spirit body. And it was only his *brain* that was defective, not his soul.'

She was so obviously startled by this theory that I marvelled how she, such an intelligent person, had never worked out the possibility of any transformation.

'You mean to imply' (she was venturing gingerly into such an untried idea) 'that my son could now be *sane*?'

'I do, indeed,' emphasising the point. 'As sane as you or I. Why not?'

She was very still. 'Sane, you said? You mean able to *think*?'

'Yes, of course. Able to think, to reason, and (deliberately) to *remember.*' Now I knew that the words were being dropped into my consciousness, either by the Brother himself, or by the Boy.

Her expression changed. Gone was the warm smile, even the hardness had vanished. At first she was incredulous; then anxiety clouded her features, and sharpened into fear.

'He could remember about his life on earth?'

I nodded. For some time she sat immovable. Only at length was her apprehension betrayed by the nervous twisting of her long, thin fingers. 'He might remember his mother, me?'

I knew that I must go carefully here, and I sent forth a prayer for help; for the right words.

'Of course he would remember you,' I hastened to assure her. 'He loved you.'

The hands were suddenly stilled. 'How could he have loved me? I hated him. He was a reproach to me, an embarrassment.'

Again, I was at a loss how to answer this. I could only leave her alone with her thoughts and the horror of her fears. Presently her mind reached out again to mine.

'I cannot understand,' she said. She stood up and began to pace about the room, keeping her face averted from me. 'If I ask the Sister, if I find that this is true. . . .' A moment later, emotion broke in her. 'Supposing it is true? Supposing he *knows* now? I mean, knows about me, about everything.' Her hands were raised to hide her face, no longer masked by arrogance and pride. 'Oh, God, don't let this happen! I am only just coming through one trial. Do not face me with another! Not my son! Not yet, oh, not yet. Have mercy. . . .'

I was silent, pity welling up in me. This poor creature and her failures. I began to think of my own omissions of compassion. I, too, had failed so many times, perhaps not in the same way as she, but in other ways, and sometimes dismally. Confrontation for all of us would never be easy. This personal application of truth left me visibly shaken. As the humble amanuensis of this saga of life and death, how much was I, too, learning? The realisation was shattering. Truth, I saw, was universal, not particular. Each one of us must carry a blotched record, which at some time would be presented for account. Thank God for the light and love which had been shown in the advanced Christocentric soul of the Brother. I tried to pray for this poor erring creature and for myself and for those I loved. When at length I recovered calmness, I saw that the Mistress had gone.

A few days later

That evening, the Polish-born pianist André Tchaikowsky was playing Fantasies on 'Music on Two', on B.B.C. 2 Television. The three Fantasies were by Mozart, Schumann and Chopin. I tuned in, turned down the lights, and settled to enjoy the beauty of the performance. It was a wonderful experience and I was caught up in the beauty of the music, as well as intrigued by the 'close-ups' of the keyboard and the hands of the pianist. His complete concentration and his oneness with his instrument were fascinating to watch and I was so enthralled that it was not until near the end of the programme that I became aware that I had a visitor, that there had been an audience of two.

For I perceived that the Mistress was sitting in the chair opposite me. She was in the same style of stiff silk dress; she still looked stately and picturesque as before, only now, her posture betrayed the deep tension of her thoughts. Her eyes were closed, her body was slightly bowed, and she was weeping.

It is the music, I told myself. It has been played with such feeling and utter beauty that it has moved her to tears. Poor soul, I thought, it must be heaven for her to listen again to harmony of sound, when she is condemned by her own self to live in sordid surroundings amongst the racket of unhappy and resentful entities, still at war with themselves and with the misery they have earned. How her sensitive musician's soul must shrink from the lack of harmony there and the wonder of it here. So closely had my emotions become linked with my unhappy visitor that I only half listened to the finale of the Chopin Fantasy.

When the programme ended, I automatically switched off the set, re-seated myself, and waited for what might ensue. 'Help her,' I prayed wordlessly. 'Help her! Please help her!'

For a while she remained silent; then, keeping her hands before her face, she burst into uncontrollable weeping.

'Oh, God,' her thoughts came clearly and sadly into my consciousness. 'He *knows*! My son knows!' She began to rock herself to and fro in a paroxysm of grief. 'I can't bear it! I can never face him! What have I done? What terrible crime have I committed against this boy, this helpless creature who was my son, whom I bore? I am so ashamed. And when we meet, what of that? For my Shining Sister has already told me we shall meet! And he is no longer deranged. He is whole and sane and in the light, whilst I am in the darkness. What will his judgement of me be? Will he censure me? Will he hate me? Oh God, why had I not been warned? Yet would I have listened? Would I ever have believed?' She became silent, weeping more within herself, utterly bereft, without hope or knowledge, drowned in the great waves of emotion that swept her. 'If only I had known. Dear God, if I could have known that Thy Law excepts no-one. If only I had had compassion.'

I was very moved. Gone was the old imperious arrogant woman; here was the soul awakened to its own judgement; here was remorse, but here was fear also. What could I do in the face of such tragedy, I who was still incarnate and fallible? I tried to think of words, of a prayer, of a hymn, a psalm, but at first nothing would come to my mind. I was beginning to become entangled in her grief, and carried away on her tide of emotion. This I knew was not my role, but I could no longer fight ciear of the tide of emotion which was swamping us both. I felt quite inadequate and although I tried to make a mental picture of the advanced soul who was her son and who felt only compassion, the screen of my mind was fogged by emotion.

This was of no use. The Mistress was unaware of me. She was closed away in her remorse, wrapped in a web of fear, and existing only in the agony of the spirit. I was identifying myself with her too passionately, identifying also with my own shortcomings in the past. I was allowing myself to be drawn too closely into her sorrow, and was becoming one with her. And by this I knew I was failing! I was inadequate. For I was allowing my personality to become disturbed, and so rendering my higher consciousness impotent. I was being drawn into the obsession of her terror and was losing my own control.

The realisation came as a shock. Suddenly, the truth came to me; I had been completely alone; I had felt shut off; the apparent reality of this terror was a net drawing me into *her* world. I knew I must pray, but my mind could think of no words. I shook physically.

Slowly, an old remembered, beloved tune flickered into my mind as if an organ played in a far distant church; then the words filtered into consciousness and I repeated them, whether correct or not I neither knew nor cared. But they were words, powerful words of Invocation:

> *Love Divine, all loves excelling,*
> *Joy of Heaven, to earth come down.*
> *Fix in us Thy humble dwelling.*
> *All Thy faithful mercies crown. . . .*

They were words of invocation to the Christ Spirit, a plea to the depth and breadth of Divine Love. They were indeed a prayer, a petition for help.

And the answer was almost immediate. A wave of peace seemed to infiltrate into the room. I felt an indescribable jar in my solar plexus region as I was thrown back from the welter of emotion. I was, somehow, returned within myself; the danger was past. Consciously I relaxed. Nerves and muscles were quietened, the pulse of my blood was calmed, thought was stilled. I ceased even to try to help. I was back in myself, the observer, the recorder, sometimes the catalyst; in my rightful place, safe and no longer being carried in an eddy of emotion towards rocks and shoals ahead.

It was then that I became aware of the change in the atmosphere even before I was conscious in my inner mind of the presence of the Boy. He stood there beside his earthly mother, a figure of light and love, and his radiance shimmered about her.

She could not see him, that I knew instinctively, but she was touched by the potency of his love. Her soul was calmed by his, and by the great power that flooded the room. As I watched, now sure of myself, and sure of God's protection, the words of another hymn that I had known well when in Canada rose into my mind. Reverently and entirely without personal emotion, I found myself misquoting it:

> *Open my eyes that I might see,*
> *Visions of Truth Thou hast for me. . . .*

It sounded inadequate; it was not a prayer for myself, although I felt I had experienced some aspect of truth. I felt it was for her, it was what this poor creature needed, to have her eyes opened, to 'see' truly.

Then, in deep meditation, I allowed the whole problem to pass from me. It would be worked out in planes of the spirit far removed from my cognisance. I was but the witness and the recorder.

When, later, I returned to my everyday consciousness, the Mistress had gone. But the Boy remained.

'My mother is progressing,' came his thought. 'Her mind will clear, and her eyes will open, as she becomes aware of my love, and no longer dreads my judgement. For love opens the way, my friend . . . love and strength to face error.'

With that he was gone.

*   *   *

Two days later, I turned on my electric fire during the dull afternoon and a face shone up at me from the artificial coals.

My fire is one of the type which has imitation logs or pieces of coal lit by a bulb underneath to represent an open hearth; the heating bars are beneath the coals. Tiny cogs, which keep turning under the made-up 'fuel', cause a flickering as though the fire was actually burning.

Yet there between the 'coals' was a face. I stared long at it. Here I must admit that the faculty of discerning faces in pictures and sometimes in trees in the country lanes is one which many people possess. Sometimes, too, I have ventured to point out such faces, and others have been able to see them also. But this was an unusual place in which to 'see' with other eyes. For between the small mounds of lighted coals was a countenance of such surpassing beauty that a thrill ran through me as I gazed. It was a young face, and yet it had an appearance of agelessness. The eyes were deep set and well apart; the cheek bones high and the forehead wide. It seemed neither completely masculine nor utterly feminine, it could be either. The expression was serene. Ribbon-like about the forehead was a band of light, and directly over the bridge of the nose, in the centre between the eyebrows, was a golden orb which gleamed even in the brightness of the countenance.

Several times I glanced away and then looked back at the fire; the face remained; gradually it resembled the idyllic face of a young man, though still retaining the feminine beauty. The eyes seemed to gaze straight at me with a deep penetrating interest.

The Brother of Light, was the thought that flashed into my mind. Yes, I decided, that is the face which was impressed upon my inner consciousness in the talks which we had had. This is the countenance of an exalted being, a messenger of Christ, a member of the Band of Light, a face that is ageless, angelic, compassionate yet strong. The light on his forehead was brighter than any electric bulb, and power seemed to stream from it to me, so that I felt I could follow this being even into the Shadow Land and yet know peace and protection.

For he is a channel, came the compelling thought, a *channel into light*, and as such he bears peace with him. The Brother of Light is a channel into light, a shepherd of sheep, a worker amongst the weak and the sinners. How glorious must be the sphere of the spirit wherein he dwells and serves his Divine

Master! How long and arduous, and yet how rewarding must have been his journey upwards into light; and what an example of hope and courage and faith for we who struggle along the Way.

The face remained for a long time. Then, still aware of this lovely presence, I was enabled to write his message. Almost as it was completed, the face died away into smudges on the coals.

'My Friend,' he began in his customary manner. 'Although your experience with the visitor from the shadows was shattering, it has served a useful purpose, in that it can be as a warning to you, as the recorder of these happenings, and to those who read these accounts, and who might be tempted to try such 'rescue' work on their own. For it illustrates the fact that any contact with those who dwell (even temporarily) in the dark regions carries risks such as you experienced. The passions and emotions of these entities are powerful and oft-times too potent for the experimenter, or even for the "do-gooder". For these entities can, and often do, fasten on to the minds of others, especially those still in the earth-world, drawing them into the welter of their own emotions, fears and terrors and their unassuaged appetites. This is the initial origin of "obsession" and "possession", a state which alters the personalities of its victims, rendering them impotent to resist temptation and evil.

'In your case, sympathy and uncontrolled emotional reaction to the Boy's mother in her tragic awakening drew you into her aura, where she could obtain strength from you. This would have meant the loss of your own identity (even if only temporarily) and would have spelt disaster, not only to your own progression but to the work you have to do. The lesson to be learnt is two-fold. In the service of healing, the personality (and this implies the emotions) has no part. Healing is an extension of the spirit only; therefore detachment from astral emotion and from the snare of sentimentality is essential in the would-be healer and helper.

'Secondly (and in your case more important), this was a

yielding to glamour, the glamour of trying to free and heal this poor entity. This, alas, blotted out the real purpose of your work, which is that of recorder and witness. You were saved by the words of invocation in the hymn that was recollected from your memory. It must be stressed again that prayer, meditation and invocation form the channel for all service. Prayer is the use of the channel to contact the Holy Spirit (God); any resulting *effects* are in the power of that Spirit alone.

'For people who wish to experiment, and those who are dazzled by the glamour of "doing-good" in the lower astral worlds, the dangers are overwhelming. They are, indeed, venturing into a den of lions without a guard at the ready to counteract attack should any of the beasts turn vicious. No helper on these planes of the spirit, however experienced, is allowed to enter the Shadow World without a higher Brother who is one of the Band of Light; or without the preparation of true prayer and a knowledge of the technique of self-protection. Pray for these poor resentful creatures that they might find peace and be led into light; but leave the *means* of their so-doing in higher hands.

'Today in the earth-world, a great danger is approaching. Mankind has reached a stage in his evolution where he is entering into the consciousness of the Fourth Dimension. This is evident from the advance in the scope of men's minds, and in the interest in the problem of time, in the exploration of space, in experimentation in telepathy, pre-cognition, extra-sensory perception and the survival of the personality after death of the physical body. Man's mind is now stretching out into exploration of his body of energy, the unseen etheric body; and for some, consciousness beyond the physical plane will be a natural outcome.

'But herein lies the element of danger. For in the projection of consciousness thus gained and the first advance towards the Spiritual Planes, the astral world of the "dead" will become more accessible to contact. This includes the astral world of ignorance and darkness with its unenlightened creatures prowling forth in search of the passions and pleasures of earth now denied them, as well as those higher regions of peace and harmony, wherein advanced souls lead pilgrims ever onward and into the planes of progress between. The danger which you are, alas, already witnessing, is to be found in the sad "obsessions" of those caught in the glamour of drugged visions, and of those already filched of their personalities by the parasitic clinging of possessive lower-astral entities. Yet, evolution progresses, God be thanked, and the light is pouring forth in the work of advanced Beings and Masters of Wisdom who are preparing groups of spiritual seekers to go forward into this great adventure.

'Caution, therefore, is necessary in this coming age. Your own experience and our warning illustrate the subtlety of such dangers. Take heed and be prepared and protected by the inner life of prayer and contemplation of the Creative Divine Spirit, aligning yourselves and your efforts within the Light of the Christ.'

*   *   *

The next evening, as I sat reading, my concentration was interrupted by the now familiar signals. There was a 'visitor'. I glanced up from the book and there across from me in the armchair sat the old woman who had been my lodger. She was smiling brightly.

'Hello! You back again?' I flashed, surprised at the return, because I had been convinced that she had gone for ever.

'I come back,' came her answering thought swiftly, 'because I got somethin' to tell you. Somethin' important!'

'Something good, I hope?' I enquired.

Her smile was most expansive; in fact her expression was completely changed from the sombre old servant who had inhabited my cottage for so long. She was serene; I felt that she had a 'satisfied' look.

'Good? Better than good!' She paused to emphasise the wonder of what she was about to impart. 'I've met *him*. Our Boy!' Her look implied the awe with which she would have

125

confronted the Queen. 'An' he's all right, 'e is. Right as you and me!' This amused me, remembering that she had once classed me as a ghost. I was indeed relieved to know that I was now 'all right'.

'You mean he is different? Not a. . . .' I caught back my thought, re-phrasing it in the language she would understand. 'Not, not . . . foolish any more?'

'Foolish? 'Im?' Here her eyes opened wide and they shone with happiness. 'Why, 'e's a prince! That's what 'e is. A prince! And beautiful. Ah, an' he thinks and talks like you an' me!'

Momentarily, I wondered how the Boy might feel at this comparison. Personally, I could never talk as he did now.

' 'E don't stay near us,' she prattled on. 'Lives in a palace, I dare say, somewhere.' She was a trifle vague. 'But he come to see me. He did. My, was I surprised, though as I says to my Mam, I ain't surprised so much at things that 'appen. You see, there's so much *more*, like, when you're dead. Like meetin' my Mam and Dad and my sister wot died when her baby was born; and there bein' no angels with wings like I learned at Sunday school. Mind, I'd like to see angels and 'arps . . . you miss 'em, somehow. I asked our Boy about 'em, and 'e said there were angels, 'e called 'em Beings, but without wings, but they were a long way off, some'ow. 'E said They shone like angels.' She pulled herself up short from the joy of reminiscing on the wonders of her heaven and returned to her subject. 'Our Boy, 'e shines too, like them Beings. He's lovely and kind. He told me 'e knew that I loved 'im and I'd looked after 'im; said 'e always knew really; only it weren't till he got,' she hesitated, 'well . . . over here, that he understood, after he was sort of . . . cured, I suppose.' Again she stopped. Her face was radiant. 'Madam, 'e thanked me! The young Master thanked me! 'e did. It made me want to cry, though now I'm glad I looked after 'im proper. I told him I was sorry about 'is being drowned, but he said that was all right, it had to happen. 'E talks clever, sometimes, an' I don't rightly understand 'im. But 'e said 'e'd forgotten it now, and anyway, it was better over this side. Fancy that, Madam! Fancy 'is bein' well and all.'

'Wonderful,' I agreed. I was touched by her simple acceptance of such miracles. Dear little soul, she had indeed 'found
her place'. My thought strayed for a moment, as I pondered
on the very obvious problem which must soon arise. The
Mistress. Almost immediately she caught my question.

'An' he knows all about the Mistress, 'is mother. 'E knows
she's been in the Shadows. And, Madam, 'e's sorry for her . . .
'is mother wot 'ated him. It could 'ave knocked me down,
hearin' that.'

'The Boy is a very advanced soul,' was the spontaneous
answer that flashed into my mind, but realising she would
not understand the meaning of this, I phrased the idea differently. I must keep her communicating. 'So he has forgiven
his mother? How wonderful!'

The old servant grew solemn. 'D'you know wot? He loves
'er, and after all she did to 'im. Loves 'er! Think of that!' She
was silent a while, still awed by this revelation. 'He said it was
all over and forgotten. And 'e wanted to help her. To help her?
When she never helped 'im! Fancy that! 'E's a saint, or an
angel, I'm sure of that.'

So she wasn't so obtuse; even her limited awareness was
capable of appreciating a fine soul. I waited.

'And wot d'you think he told me? That I 'ad to forgive 'er,
too. Me? He said it would help 'er to "go on", and me too!'

I sent out a strong thought that she would be able to
accomplish this act of love. 'If *he* can, you can,' I tried to
prompt.

'Me? After all she done? After me 'ating her for years?'
She shook herself sadly. 'That's wot's queer about bein' dead.
You got to forgive folks.'

I considered this, sending out a call for the right words to
say. They seemed to flash right into my mind; again I knew
that I was in touch with greater than I. 'Yes, but my dear,
you've found your way. You've been guided to those who love
you, haven't you? Surely, *you* can show gratitude by forgiving
this poor creature, as her son has done. Besides, she is probably
very sorry now.'

127

The concept of the Mistress as a 'poor creature' seemed to amuse the former servant. I was beginning to discover that my 'old woman' was very 'normal' in our earthly translation of that word; also that she possessed a fundamental sense of humour, which was most redeeming.

'Coo! That 'ud burn her if she heard that!' came the light-hearted response. 'A poor crittur? It don't seem possible; but then so many things don't seem possible now. 'Er with her grand clothes, an' 'er grand ways! But you're right, Madam. Our Boy said the same thing. I got to be grateful, oh, I see that.'

'And you will try to be kind to her?' I asked.

Her decision came slowly, almost reluctantly. 'I'll try, Madam. I told Boy that. I said I'd try.' Then with the faintest of grins, she added. 'After all, I ain't got to do wot *she* says anymore!'

She was still very human! So the personality does survive death, but to be changed and refined and gentled by love.

'And you will help her?'

This took her by surprise. 'Me? Help her? Wot can *I* do for her?'

Again came the words flashing to me. 'You can show her that love is stronger than hate.'

She watched me closely. 'It ain't goin' to be easy,' she admitted truthfully. 'But I'll try, Madam. I got to do that for our Boy's sake.'

And your own, and for your Father, Who is Love, I wanted to add. But this might be felt as preaching. All I flashed back, happily, was 'I'm glad. It will be all right, you see.'

'Yes, Madam. Our Boy said I got to meet 'er, but 'e said she'd be different-like.' Again the faint grin. 'That'll be worth seein'.'

'I'm sure it will make it easier,' I ventured. 'And you really do want to help her get out of the dreary place she is in.'

The thin lips were pursed. 'I . . . suppose I do. I'll try, you see, I am thankful, like you said,' she broke off embarrassed.

'That's the spirit,' I cheered; then I too grinned to myself.

She picked up my amusement swiftly.

'It's queer bein' a spirit, Madam. I ain't truly got used to it yet. But it's nicer than bein' on earth. Even, begging your pardon, in me cottage.'

'Bless you!' The thought framed itself with real sincerity.

'Don't know if I can come back again, Madam. Only I wanted to tell you about 'im, an' about 'er, an' about me. I'm 'appy, Madam. Expect you know that now, real 'appy.'

'Thank God,' I murmured to myself. But whether she registered this, I do not know. She was already gone.

CHAPTER NINE

The Purpose Fulfilled

In January of 1973, I had an operation on my hip and was in hospital and in a nursing home for nearly six weeks. It was an ordeal, and, although my body healed swiftly and perfectly, I found that I was not able to concentrate in my mind on any subject for any length of time. Hence I found it impossible to write, and this book of recordings was put aside. Indeed, as the spring moved on, I began to think that the whole project would be shelved. Perhaps I had mistaken my role of recorder; perhaps it had all been a figment of my imagination. I decided to forget the story until I was recovered.

But I was not allowed to forgo it entirely. For one evening late in March, the 'atmosphere' in my cottage lifted into a light and peace that held me quiescent, and I knew that the high soul whom I recognised as a 'Brother of Light' was contacting my mind. I reached for a notebook, and recorded His thoughts.

'Dear Friend, the channel of your mind seems, at the moment, to be choked, and your work as amanuensis for this astral drama to which you have been a witness, appears to you to have been shelved. Yet this is not so. The drama of remorse of the Mistress is working itself out in a level of consciousness beyond time as you conceive of it; and a higher part of you, your soul, has been in contact with this entity, even during these weeks of apparent cessation of effort.

'My Friend, nothing ceases; all is continual advancement. All is evolution, in your earthly world of dense matter, through all levels of consciousness, even to the Divine state of *seeming* inactivity. Thus, though to you we have not been at communicating level, i.e. your "conscious" level, there has been no waste of effort, no cessation of progress. All has proceeded in order. With returning physical strength and mental confidence, you will be enabled to take up the work again and to record as before. Only now, perhaps, after your own sufferings, you will do so with a deeper awareness, a clearer sense of dedication and a greater understanding of the use and purpose of the channel.'

There was no more, but I felt comforted and uplifted. The work would go on, indeed, *was* going on. I could only stand and wait and remember that time was not, and evolution was ceaseless.

April 18th

Time had passed since I had added any account of experience to this record, for my channel of awareness had been closed down. I was entirely unaware of any 'visitors' to my cottage from another world. I was deprived of inspiration so necessary to a writer, and consequently life (creative life) was dead in me. I had become the victim of that depression so dreaded by a writer, the fallow period.

There was, however, an experience which I still retained in my memory and which often intruded itself into my thoughts. It was the recollection of a painful contact which had occurred only two days before I had entered hospital in January, a contact which took place in daylight, in the mid-morning and which I had never been able to record. Usually any 'visitations' happened during the evenings when I was quiet and not occupied with household chores. But this strange 'tuning in' had happened about eleven o'clock in the morning, when I was busy about household duties.

With an inexplicable suddenness, my mood had dropped from peace to misery. I paced restlessly up and down my sun-filled room, for the day was bright for January and pale sunshine streamed in and touched the furniture with gold. I was unhappy, so unhappy that tears welled up into my eyes. I felt as if the whole substance of my world had been caught up in some terrible freak storm and washed from under me, so that

I no longer knew the firm comfort of Mother Earth, but was poised somewhere in space, lost, uncertain and frightened. I found myself saying, 'Please help me! Please help me! I am frightened. I am lost! I cannot bear it any longer. I am sorry for all I did. It was all terrible and I am miserable. Oh God, if there is a God, forgive me.'

Then I knew that this was a contact with the mind of the Mistress. Not that this knowledge made much difference, though the tension relaxed a little. The poor woman seemed to have insinuated herself even into my aura and I, too, was possessed by her remorse. It was a ghastly experience and one I wish never to go through again. This was one-ness with a soul in torment; this was shared misery to such an extent that I, too, confessed my own faults and, with her, asked God's forgiveness. I knelt beside my warm fire, and poured my whole soul, with hers, out to the mercy of the Creator. I found myself praying for her, for myself and for all sinners.

Presently, I rose and going to the case of gramophone records, I selected one that was a great favourite of mine and that had been lent to me by a friend. It is Elgar's Sacred Music, played and sung by the choir in Worcester Cathedral. Softly, the boys' voices filled the room in the beautiful Ave Verum. I was calmed and the misery of the last half-hour left me. I sat down, closed my eyes, and speaking in whispers, I recited the twenty-third psalm.

'Help her,' I beseeched and now I knew that I was free of this nightmare of remorse. 'Help her to find the Light.'

It seemed a long time before I was restored sufficiently to get up and go about my business. But at length the atmosphere was cleared, the poor, unquiet spirit was gone and I lit a taper of incense. I must write this tonight, I told myself, while it is still fresh in my memory, because it is important. It is a step in the return of a wayward one to the Father; it is the purging of a personality as the soul calls it towards the light.

That evening, I had scarcely sat down to write my experiences of the morning, when the telephone bell rang. The call was from the hospital. 'Can you come in, in two days' time?'

asked a pleasant voice. 'Your operation would be the next day.'

The news paid finish to my intention to write. I was too busy preparing, telephoning, writing notes and packing my bags to find time to set my remembrances on paper; besides, my mind was in its own turmoil. Now, I was facing my own ordeal. The Mistress's agony was not recorded and, until this moment, three months' later, I had resolutely put it from my mind. Perhaps it is better that way; time has softened the impact and, as the Brother of Light has informed me, the penitence of the Mistress has pursued its course and, no doubt, now will be less painful.

Easter Monday

I returned home in the afternoon from a visit to a friend. The weather was cold and wet and the sky was dark. By seven o'clock I was comfortably ensconced in an armchair before the electric fire in the inglenook, the curtains were drawn to shut out the dreary evening and the lamps were cosily alight.

I picked up a book which I had started to read and was absorbed in it. I felt relaxed and at peace. But presently, across the concentration of my mind, stole a feeling of purposefulness. I set aside the book, and gave myself to the atmosphere of love and beauty that filled the cottage. The Brother of Light, I thought with thanksgiving, and rested in the joy and one-ness of his presence.

There was no communication. My mind registered nothing but the enlightened feeling of his extended consciousness. My notebook remained untouched. I thought of a friend, whose mind was then in turmoil, and asked that the comfort of this love might be transmitted. I was still, in silent communion.

Slowly, I grew aware that another visitor had become focused in my cottage sitting room. The Mistress! She is here. She has come back, flashed through my thought, and with some trepidation, recalling the agony of her last contact, I waited. Gently, almost imperceptibly, she became apparent to my inner sight. She was sitting in the armchair opposite me, a very different apparition from the distraught entity who had knelt with me, and wept her remorse, on that memorable morning in January. She seemed calm, and although she still appeared to wear a stiff silk dress, such as was fashionable in her time, it was no longer black, and unrelieved by any light touches, such as I had seen before. Now, it appeared to me to be blue, a deep midnight blue, which shimmered, as though shot with gold, when she moved. She is very beautiful, I thought, sensing a subtle change about her. I waited.

As soon as my attention had been completely caught by her, she began to transmit thought to me. 'I have been brought to see you,' she began, and the arrogance had left her thought. 'I am told that you will understand.'

'I will understand,' I flashed back, 'for I, too, have been through trouble and through a cleansing.'

'A cleansing?' She seemed to savour the meaning of the word. 'I suppose that is what you might call my own experiences ... a cleansing?'

I remained silent, waiting for further information. The Brother of Light was now conscious to my inner sight, as he stood beyond the Mistress. Yet she was quite obviously unaware of any other presence in the room, even though the light from him rayed out to her form.

'Yet,' she mused, 'the experience was more of an acceptance.' She hesitated.

'Acceptance of what?' I prompted. I knew that I must draw her out as much as possible. The inexplicable impression of being, or at least of enacting, the role of priest to a penitent came to me, so that I became confused, almost self-conscious and thus nearly broke the contact. Yet, again, the strength of the Light Brother held me to the work to be accomplished. 'Acceptance of what?' I repeated, though now I felt I knew.

'Acceptance of that which I have done, during the time I was on earth.' The words came simply from her mind to mine. 'Acceptance of my own guilt. Acknowledgement that I have hurt others, terribly.'

134

'Me, too,' I responded with the sadness of recalling difficult passages in my own life.

'You?' Her astonishment was obvious. 'But you are not dead. You are not . . . over here. How can you see yourself as you really are?'

I felt the Brother's thought echo through me. 'We do not have to wait for death to be shown the results of our actions.' They were his words, not mine; yet I, too, could shudder at soul-scars that still ached.

She was silent and withdrawn for a while, apparently examining this statement.

'If only I had known!' It was a whispered thought, yet it rang through my soul as a wail of the despair and misery that must echo down the ages of man's slow evolution into understanding and truth. 'If only I had known! I believe, truly I am of the persuasion that I could have changed then, I could have altered myself.'

'Could you?' Now, I was consciously following the instruction of the Brother of Light. 'Were you not so enclosed and wrapped in selfishness that you were unaware of the harm you did?'

She seized on this, as a drowning man on a wooden spar. 'Then I cannot be altogether *blamed*, can I?'

This was a knotty question. I answered with caution. '*Nobody* blamed you. You accused yourself, though only after your inner eyes were opened and you *saw*.'

She drew back into silence and meditation, and it was as though she sighed inwardly.

'You mean by that . . . after I had been made to live in that terrible place? You are telling me that it took the horror of being in contact with others who in their lives had been hard and cruel, even brutal, and were still the same, to show me myself?'

'Perhaps it made you hate what you saw in others, yet never realised in yourself, so that you longed to change, to find peace of mind and soul.'

Her hands went up swiftly to cover her face. 'I prayed,' she confessed. 'I prayed to God, as I had never done before. I asked forgiveness for some of the things I had done. I still don't know whether there is a God, or even a Saviour, yet I prayed.'

There was a long silence and stillness between us. I scarcely trusted myself to think, knowing that my visitor might pick up my thoughts, and these must, at all costs, be positive and helpful.

At last I sent forth, 'And you received an answer from God?' She shook her head. 'I do not know whence the answer came.'

'He sent a Sister of Light to you, even when you thought yourself in hell?'

Now she wept. 'It is true. The lovely Sister came. She gave me hope, after I had almost lost all. She helped me to leave that awful place and she brought me here, where once again I could listen to the music that I loved and see flowers and . . . and beautiful things. And often she talked with me. I am sure she is an angel of God. Then I met a Brother. He filled my soul with awe, yet he is indeed wonderful. Could he have been a messenger of God? Is that possible? Could they have been God's answer?'

I pondered for a while, awaiting inspiration from the Brother of Light. 'They must have come from some loving Father to help you,' I suggested. 'But you needed love *and* correction. Could we not say that they held up a mirror that you might see yourself as you truly were, that you might be inspired to *change* that image?'

She shuddered. 'That is just what they did! It was hell itself. I went through a hell of remorse! Never again, never again, please God, such a hell, such an agony of unmasking.'

I could well agree, recalling that morning before my operation, when her grief and repentance had seeped into my soul and we had become united in a despair that scorched to the depths of my being.

She appeared to sway to and fro and her thoughts came slowly, hesitatingly. Once or twice she wept, as truth welling up in her emphasised her words.

'I did not know how much I made others suffer . . . yet perhaps that is not true either. For I was critical and unloving and the cruelty in me was fed and satisfied when I made others squirm. But consciously I would never admit to it. I thought I was ill-used, that fate was loaded against me, so maybe I vented my spite on others less able to retaliate. I believed myself to be just, though severe. I could not see.'

'We don't *want* to see. We refuse to acknowledge.' I found that I was whispering the words painfully to myself, for it seemed that in this sharing I, too, was on trial. I knew I must face the faults still pushed down beneath the cloak of egotism and glamour that was the personality with which I faced the world. With this distraught soul I was gazing into the mirror of self.

As if she was cognisant of our one-ness in this confrontation, the Mistress raised her head and looked straight at me.

'So this could happen before death, as well as after? Is that the Church's teaching on redemption?'

'Repentance has always been the way to Heaven,' I felt that this was a lame explanation for religion, and I flushed with embarrassment. But immediately the words of the Shining One who was watching us echoed through me, 'Better by far that repentance and the new birth should come to us *before* our release from the world of matter. Is it not wiser to cast off such burdens of guilt *before* the soul leaves its house of flesh? To approach the next stage of life still blinded by self-conceit is like hauling dirt into a beautiful room. Are you surprised that at least a measure of the dirt must be reduced to nothingness before the doors to the stately home are flung wide for your entry? Does it astonish you that there are places where such cleansing must take place, such a place as you have yourself occupied?' I gasped as the Brother's words swept through me. How apt was their message not only to the recorder whose mind registered it and to the penitent who was accepting it, but also for those who, with discernment, would later read it. 'Repentance and a new beginning have long been the key to open doors to a fuller, more rewarding

137

life on the earth plane. Should there be divergence here from such a law, here where the inhabitants are even more clearly shown *as they are* and not as they pretend to be? Without the veil of the flesh, there is no mask 'twixt thee and me.'

As the echo of these words died in my mind, I was held in the power of his thought. I sat on in silence, daring neither to think nor speak. All was stillness. The very air of the room seemed arrested. Time stood still. Eternity was.

Cars passed outside; a hooter sounded; a laugh echoed along the street, a dog barked. Yet within these old walls there was the silence and the awe of truth. With a new humility, the Mistress went on to her knees and bowed her head.

'Oh, Christ of mercy,' she moaned, 'forgive me for what I did to my poor demented son.'

I felt I could take no more. I closed my eyes, and leaned back in my chair, spent and too tired even to record. When at last I was able to concentrate in my inner sight, I discovered that the Mistress had gone; and that the translucent light in which had stood the Wise One was now withdrawn.

Next day

That night, after I had settled myself in bed with a book to read myself to sleep, I became startlingly aware of the presence of the Boy. This time I could not 'see' him even with my inner sight, but I knew the beauty of his presence. The words of his message seemed to steal gently into my mind. I had no time to get pad and pen, so I concentrated hard, knowing that I must try to remember all that was communicated in order to write it later for the book.

'You have received my poor mother,' he began, 'I was not able to be present with you then, yet my thought and prayer were tuned to you both. I also was aware that my Brother was with you and with my mother.

'Poor soul! She suffers. She is awakened and she is sad. I, who love her, can scarcely bear to picture her enduring the misery amongst such unawakened and often vicious entities. Neither can I accept, for one who was ever elegant, refined and a lover of beauty, the dark hovel that she believes she now inhabits. I long to see her move into the Light. My prayer, always, is for the peace of her soul. Pray, too, for her, my friend; pray that her inner sight may be cleared. Pray that the errors of her earthly existence may be transmuted from transgression into steps of progress. Pray with me that her soul may rise triumphant from the torn and tortured remnants of her personality that still cling about her. She has indeed begun the casting off of those "unclean garments" with which she crossed over into this life. But there is more to be done. She herself must gather these relics of emotional failures and with the kindred flame of newly awakened love burn them from her consciousness.

'Already she has felt remorse concerning her treatment of the child I was when on earth. Remorse and acceptance! Yes, my friend, powerful kindling for this fire of Love. But the flame itself can arise only from the Divinity within her soul. It is there, even though choked by the stones of bitterness and the ashes of dead passions, for divinity is in every entity however depraved and egoistic and blinded by materialism and glamour. The light of divinity shines through the personality mask when those materialistic concepts of human existence are recognised for the illusion that they are. For such example to the human race have saints and sages and masters sacrificed themselves in all ages, even to the greatest Master Himself.

'To bring the divine understanding to mankind is the aim and desire of all here in this spiritual world who have progressed into light. To awaken light in dark souls already released from the flesh, but not the fleshly emotions and failures, is the task of many advanced pilgrims here. Light is kindled by love, and it is such love that needs to be aroused in my poor mother.

'For this we ask help and prayer; and not for this dear soul alone, but for others also, who still dwell in darkness, incarcerated in those prison cells which they themselves have created.'

Here I found my thoughts wandering to the strange statement concerning 'burning of unclean garments from the newly awakened soul'. A question formed itself in my mind and immediately the answer came.

'In my mother's case, as indeed in all cases,' was the Boy's explanation, 'there will be confrontation. My mother will be brought to face those she has wronged or hurt, those she has hated, her earthly husband, the son she despised, the maid she bullied and crushed, as well as others; and only by love can she resolve the damage she has done.'

Poor creature, I thought, and my soul shuddered for its own past mistakes.

'Yes, indeed, but the law is just,' the Boy knew my thought. 'You will witness how Love heals the wounds even as it burns away the memories of dark emotions.'

Concentration flickered, and the message ended. There was no more but before I slept I wondered about the question of innocence and ignorance in the world, and although I felt more than diffident about the reactions which this book might arouse in the general public, I knew that I had no right to withhold its truth. I had not asked for this work, nor for these revelations. The knowledge had not been mine. Therefore, I had no jurisdiction over it. If, as I believed, this was truth, and it had been communicated to me in its right time, then in its right time it must go forth to be accepted or rejected and, as I hoped, to bring understanding, hope and light to those who read.

May

That same strange 'listening' silence swept so strongly across my concentration on the modern book I was reading, that I had perforce to put it down. Printed words no longer made sense. Power was in the little sitting room, the power of the Spirit, and this time I was aware of apprehension and trembling within me. Almost as an automaton, I went across the room and selected the favourite record of the *Sacred Music* of Elgar, sung by the choir of Worcester Cathedral. I set it revolving on the turn-table of my record player and stood listening as the boys' clear high voices filled the room. Suddenly I shivered, even though this was early May and sunshine filtered through the net curtains. I stood by the radiator to warm myself, even though I knew that it was not my body that was recording the chill, but my mind, which had been tried enough by the intimacy of these astral emotions. For I was quite cognisant of the purpose of this visitation; I was to be the scribe and the participator in the climax of confrontation that was even now being enacted, out of time and space, such as my mind accepted, by creatures of another world, another consciousness. I tried to push away the insistent thoughts by concentrating on the music and anchoring my awareness more firmly in this material world, but it was of no use. I *knew* that my inner self was opened and already that I was functioning out of time and space. Immediately, words poured into my consciousness, snatches of conversation and, with the recognition of this switch of awareness, I was back in my seat, pen and pad in readiness and all former apprehension dissolved. The scene had begun.

I was aware of the Mistress first. She was seated in the chair opposite me, just as though she had occupied it all the day through. As if, indeed, it was *her* chair and her home. She was different from the restless creature who had prowled about, touching my furniture, for now she appeared calm and she remained still. For the first time, I was aware of an aura of gentleness about her. Beyond her, standing near the wall, was her son, the Boy. He wore the dark rough habit of a friar, with a band of white about his waist. From within and about him shone a light that was pure and white and shimmering. The light beamed out and touched the form of the mother in the chair, yet she was not conscious of it. I thought how wonderful was this love that blessed his mother and afforded strength for her trials.

Suddenly, it seemed that my attention was caught by a flicker of movement across the room. There was present another entity and, as my thought registered this, I saw, to my surprise and consternation, the form of my erstwhile lodger, the little old servant woman. She seemed quite at ease, and, except that she no longer wore her apron (and I concluded this must be by her own choice), she was the same neat little figure in her long-skirted dress, only now she no longer fidgeted with her hands but remained relaxed and at peace. She took no notice whatsoever of me, obviously intent on the task she had returned to perform; and she kept her gaze on her Mistress. Her face expressed pleasurable surprise, more than anything else; then, as she turned towards the Boy, a look of utter love and joy flashed across it. The Boy looked at her, and his smile was warm and encouraging. To me, watching, I could have sworn that a golden shaft of light flowed from him to her and was returned by the woman deepened by the glowing colours of love.

I felt my nerves tighten, and such was my depth of concentration that had a fire arisen in the material structure of the cottage, I believe I would have been quite impervious to any danger or possible damage. All I could do was to hold myself in a state of suspension, awaiting events. Would these two opposing entities see each other? Would the new serenity in both of them evaporate as old hates, old fears, old angers rose again to confront them? Was this, indeed, the confrontation of which I had been warned? I could but wait and watch, too involved even to pray or to send forth a peaceful radiation. Not that I feel now that efforts of mine were needed. I was outside this triangle of love and hate; I was but the audience in this drama, and all the needed power was throbbing between them; this was the Divine Power of Love-Wisdom, far beyond our earthly conception. A warmth of contentment enveloped me. All was well. All would be well. I began to write my notes describing the scene.

The Mistress, turning as she caught the movement of another form, faced her one-time maid, the girl who, from adolescence, she had bullied and enslaved, now an old woman and evidently in the similar predicament, that is, dead to the world of matter.

'You?' thought flew from her like sparks. 'What are you doing here?'

The old woman seemed to shrink to even smaller proportions.

For a second of my time, I felt, rather than saw, the fear arise in her eyes.

'I used to live here, Madam.'

'*You* lived here?' The Mistress stared aghast. 'Here?'

'Yes, Madam, for a long time.' The servant was now more controlled; 'I came 'ere, if you remember, after . . . after you . . . died!' The last thought was a gulp of emotion.

There was a lull. The face of the Mistress expressed sudden horror, as remembrance of the Shadows returned. 'After I . . . died?' With an effort she appeared to be controlling herself. 'Of course. And you?' Now she looked with open curiosity at her one-time servant. 'Did you die also?'

'Yes, Madam, I died too. I was old, you see, Madam.'

'You were old? And after? You went . . . where?'

'I . . . didn't go to 'ell, Madam?' Was there a certain satisfaction in expressing her position to one whom she knew had been in hell? I could not tell. 'I stayed here, in the cottage.' Now the words and thoughts came with a rush. Perhaps she regretted the small lapse. 'I stayed 'ere for a very long time, so they told me; years an' years. I was lost, Madam. Lost.'

A gleam seemed to be reflected in the countenance of the Mistress.

'I'm not surprised at that. You were never very bright, I recall.' To me, watching, a light seemed to flash from the Boy in the corner of the room; it encircled the spirit form of his mother, and remained stationary about her. She paused. Perhaps she was recollecting her own position. She shuddered. 'But, at least, you have never known the sheer horror of what *I* have been through.'

'No, Madam.' Now there was open sympathy in the face of the old woman. 'I did 'ear you were in the Shadow Lands.'

Resentment and arrogance flared again in the younger woman. Her foot tapped impatiently. 'Shadow Lands? Is that what you call them? It was hell, I tell you, hell!' The light gleamed about her. Suddenly, she put up her hands and covered her face. 'I have been in hell.' There was a long silence. I wrote steadily. The Mistress sobbed. Now she had come full circle in

143

her humiliation; that her stupid one-time slave should have escaped a fate such as hers, even though she had been lost, as she said, was almost unbelievable. In a burst of remorse, she flung out, 'Was I really *that* bad? Did I deserve such a fate? Tell me, did I?'

The gaze of the old woman turned with instinctive trust to the Boy. She watched his face, and I was certain that a telepathic thought was transferred from him to her. Was it her answer?

'You weren't that bad, Madam. Least, it don't seem so bad, now.'

The Mistress was silent, mulling this over in her mind.

'Perhaps it doesn't, now that we're dead.' Then she swung round, avoiding the servant's watchful eyes. 'But you hated me, didn't you? I was cruel to you. I loved power over people, and you were always so afraid of me.'

With rising apprehension, I awaited the servant's reply, expecting in my ignorance that the dark emotion of a lifetime would break forth again. Nothing happened. I glanced at the Boy. He was standing, immovable and clothed in light. Now he stretched out his hand towards the humble creature who had been kind to him. From his fingers, I sensed, more than saw, the beam of light dart across the room; then from the palm of his hand it seemed to me that a great warmth like a glowing fire of love spread across the cottage room and lit the figure of the maid.

'I don't 'ate you now, Madam,' she sent out, and I was astonished at the new serenity in her. 'I'll never 'ate you no more, Madam.'

The Mistress sobbed unrestrainedly. Presently, she raised her head. Slowly, she turned and looked at her old servant.

'Why?' she asked, wondering. 'Why won't you hate me?'

My old lodger woman looked puzzled. 'I don't rightly know, Madam, not rightly, I don't. Only, only, it don't seem to matter no more. I mean . . . now I found my way.'

'Your way?' Her Mistress seemed utterly overcome. 'Where?'

'My way to my Dad and Mam, Madam. I'm with them

now. It's a kind of 'eaven, it is. So beautiful, flowers and trees and . . . and light. An' people are kind to each other. I mean, spirits are kind. . . .' She broke off embarrassed.

'Spirits?'

'Yes, Madam,' the old woman was eager to show her knowledge. 'Spirits. Least, that's what they tells me we are. We ain't people no more.'

'Spirits?' Her Mistress echoed the thought. 'I never believed in spirits when, when I was . . . alive.' Her fingers twisted and twined about each other. 'To think I have become a spirit.' She was quiet for some while. Suddenly her thought flashed across to her visitor, 'Why have you come here?'

The servant hesitated, gazing appealingly at the Boy.

'Because,' now she appeared to be repeating words flashed from him. 'You . . . called me, Madam.'

'*I* called you?'

'Yes, Madam.' At first the explanation came lingeringly, then as assurance grew, with impressive integrity. 'It all come about in a queer sort of way. I . . . I saw your face, Madam, quite plain, I did, an' you looked unhappy. I told my Mam. She says, "You go an' talk to 'er. Tell her 'ow sorry you are for her . . . and for 'ating her." '

'Sorry? You are sorry for me?' This was almost too much. 'For me? After my treatment of you? I never thought kindly of you. It never occurred to me that you might have feelings, or that I owed you anything.' The brittleness broke in her. Perhaps for the first time, she was aware that she was speaking absolute truth. But now it was as if she could not stop. 'You worked for me. I treated you worse than I would have treated a dog. And you are sorry for me? Because I have been in hell? Oh, God, where am I? What has happened to us both? What is this place that I cannot mask my shame? Must I be humiliated by your pity, too?' She wept.

The servant looked puzzled and fearful; this was not what she had intended. 'Don't be angry with me, Madam. I'm only sorry because you are suffering. An' . . . an' I'm too happy to want you to be sad. I don't want that nobody should be hurt, honest I don't. Not any more. Look, I'll say I'm sorry I hated you once, because I did. But that's all over now. We've left it behind us, ain't we? I mean, now we're dead.'

The Mistress shook her head. 'I have not left it behind me. You may have done. I have to live amongst it; be with others who are coarse and cruel and who still hate.' She shuddered.

Again, I saw the servant plead for inspiration from the Boy. This time he smiled, seeming to express that the conversation was going exactly as he intended. The look that passed between them was one of understanding and compassion, and their thoughts seemed to touch and mingle as colours in a kaleidoscope. The old woman was immediately sustained and strengthened.

'But you don't 'ave to stay there, Madam, not if you really don't want to. My Mam says, an' she's been 'ere for ages, so she should know . . . that if you're really sorry, an' . . . an' you changes yourself, that you can be shown the way to the better land, like I was.' She paused, then bravely plunged on, 'I means, change your thoughts about . . . about people, an' forgive 'em, as they forgive you. That's in the prayer, ain't it? . . . about the Kingdom of Heaven. You have to think different over 'ere, Madam. I mean about your husband, the Master, and . . . your son.'

The Mistress swung round facing the Boy, yet it was obvious that as yet she could not see him.

'My son? That poor fool?'

' 'E ain't a poor fool, Madam. That Boy's an angel. He's beautiful, an' he loves you.'

'Loves me? After. . . . ?'

'He does, Madam, an' he wants to 'elp you, to take you out of . . . of. . . .'

'Of hell? My son does? How can you know this?'

Now the servant was almost triumphant. 'Because I see him, Madam. I see 'im many times, an' he told me so.'

'You have seen my son?'

'I have,' nodding vigorously.

'And is he. . . ?'

'I tell you 'e's an angel, an' right as you an' me.'

'My demented son right? Is it possible?'

The servant flashed a glance of pure joy at the advanced Spirit standing silently, watching.

'See for yourself, Madam. He's 'ere. Your son's 'ere. He's 'ere, now.' She pointed to the corner of the room, where the light glowed in unearthly brilliance.

Slowly, the Mistress turned herself and stared at the direction in which her maidservant pointed. For some minutes she gazed, terrified, and I stopped writing, and held my breath.

'Here?' it was a mental cry of fear, and yet hope. 'Here . . . now?' She stared for a long time, then, as if her sight had suddenly cleared, and she could scarcely bear it, she put her hands up to her face, and covered her eyes. 'That is my son? But that is an angel, an angel of Light.'

The love and compassion in the Boy's expression was almost more than I could bear. I, too, closed my eyes, and sat back in the chair, overcome by this glimpse into another world, out of time and space; and this example of Love in its highest form.

'Mother!' The Boy stretched out his hands, and light enveloped them both, as the woman gazed at him in awe and remorse.

There was absolute silence and stillness, and power filled the cottage room, the power of the Spirit. Slowly, the woman slipped to her knees before the light bearer who had been her earthly son, despised and rejected. She closed her eyes and clasped her hands, in the fervour of the first prayer she had ever purposefully uttered.

'*Our Father*,' the words came across to my mind clearly and powerfully. '*Who art in Heaven, Hallowed be Thy Name. Thy Kingdom come . . .*' here she faltered, remorse and repentance choking her. '*Forgive us our trespasses as we forgive those who trespass against us . . .*' again a pregnant silence. '*As they forgive us, who have trespassed against them. . . . Deliver us from evil . . .* from the evil of the Shadows, Oh God . . . from the evil in ourselves . . . from the evil we have done. . . . *For Thine is*

147

the Kingdom.' Now she was weeping openly. 'In Thy mercy, forgive me, Father and let me into Thy Kingdom. Amen.'

I could scarcely breathe. The room was so still; it seemed filled with a translucent light. I, too, was moved to tears. The Boy stepped forward and took the clasped hands between his own, as the old servant with a loving gesture, gently touched the bowed shoulders. Then she moved to the door and somehow she was gone.

I closed my eyes, and for a short out-of-time moment, I found myself living the woman's agony of repentance with her. Without realising what I was saying, I was reciting the twenty-third Psalm, using a translation of my own to fit the case.

> *The Lord is her Shepherd,*
> *Therefore shall she lack nothing.*
> *He leadeth her beside the still waters*
> *He restoreth her soul.*

When, at length, I returned to consciousness of the material world in which I had my habitation, I saw that the room was empty; my visitors from beyond death had gone. The cottage felt strangely empty.

Love had visited us. Love had come down to us. And love was dissolving and healing the hurts of hatred for ever. Truly I and the cottage were blessed.

Next day

The Brother of Light brought the blessing of his presence.

'My Friend,' he began, and my mind leapt to listen to his words. 'You have witnessed the miracle of the power of Love, the cleansing and purging of the lower emotions by the force which is the creative power by which and in which we are all One.

'But you have been a witness to much more, and this we wish you to stress in your recordings, for it is of great moment and may bring much understanding to those who read with the "open eye". Heaven and hell are states of consciousness here as much as they are on your earthly planet; and each entity, after he has passed through the experience of death of the physical body, brings with him here that state of consciousness which he had attained for himself whilst in incarnation in matter; and here he will dwell in that consciousness for as long as such level persists.

'However, evolution is still a law here, as it is in your world. The soul is continually evolving. In your material, limited consciousness, evolution proceeds by the creating of thought-forms, sometimes for upliftment of the individual or the race, sometimes for the recording of beauty, sometimes for the development of compassion for one's fellows; but, sometimes, alas, force is given to forms of destruction by employing the negative use of emotions. Thought brings energy, which builds form. Evolution uses the form, works for it, lives in it, and manifests through it until its precepts are established. Then the form must be broken. This is essential, for its service is finished, and a new form has to be evolved. "Break down and rebuild", has ever been a law of evolution, as you will realise as you look back and search the history records of your planet. Break the worn-out form to create the new.

'In this drama, you have been shown how two entities after their souls had left their physical bodies, remained closed in the thought-forms they had created. And for as long as they persisted in holding to these forms of thought, so were they aliens to the new state of consciousness required for true living here; and thus they were unable to progress onward.

'Witness your "lodger" in your cottage, a poor soul completely shut away in materialism, and even that materialism only of the lowest aspiration to receive the "crumbs" from the rich woman's table. She was a creature eager only for physical well-being which her life had denied her, and she had spilt the precious gift of thought in envying and hating the Mistress she served. Whether this slavery was karmic in her case, is beyond the point; definite energy spent in envy and hatred held her prisoner and chained her to the very person she was forced to serve.

'After the death of her body in old age, the form she had

created still clung so close about her soul that she continued to dwell in it, shut away from everything but her own limited imagination. The pathetic tumble-down cottage, as it then was, was all she knew, or *wanted to know*. And this level of aspiration had persisted for many of your earth years.

'Yet it was essential to break that form and release her, that she might learn a new state of awareness and take her first tentative steps into this new world to which she had been introduced by the disintegration of the physical form which housed her soul. So limited, we knew, was her thought and experience, that "awakening" would be painful. Confidence and love, so necessary for her soul-health, must come to her through those she trusted . . . the Boy, her earthly father and her mother, and through converse with a stranger (yourself) who had developed the faculty of contact out of the three dimensions of time and space.

'This, indeed, has now been accomplished, as you know and a "lamb" who was lost now brought again to the Way.

'In like manner, the Mistress had imprisoned herself by arrogance, hatred and cruelty, wasting the precious substance of mind to fashion a concrete form that imprisoned her soul. Here let me stress that the soul of this creature is fine and sensitive to beauty, ready to accept the divine as beauty. Yet, with this dark shadow of a shell she had created, she entered her new existence. She brought her hell with her, a hell so potent with evil that escape seemed impossible; and there she remained to wither in misery.

'But love, in the soul of her son whom she had despised, sought to break the shell about her and after much endeavour he has succeeded. At last, this form of negation has been destroyed, as it needed to be, and the hurts will be dissolved by love. The entity can now enter this new thought-world, and create, by love, that beauty which still lives in her soul.

'It is a moving story and, alas, so unnecessary and yet so often repeated. "The evil that men do lives after them, the good is often interred in their bones," as your poet writes, has some meaning here, for the evil carries on until its form is smashed, whilst the good, often deeply ingrained, creates in itself a more glorious form.

'If readers apprehend the lessons to be gathered from these examples of thought-form prisoners, this story will not have been in vain. Man is body, soul and spirit. Body, with all its selfish emotions, cannot exist here, where progress is carried on in the mind towards re-union with the soul. The time to shatter those illusions of earth-life, of separativeness, to overcome disharmony of thought and emotion, is during the sojourn on the planet earth, not after the transition to the Astral and Spiritual worlds brought about by what you call death.'

Late May

Spring had come in swiftly and lit the cottage with light and sunshine. In my tiny garden I had spread the deckchair and had lounged happily all afternoon, reading. Coming through the back door into my living room, in late afternoon, I was immediately conscious of the Mistress standing quietly by the window, and beside her the son she had rejected on earth. I stopped. Somehow I felt an intruder, for such was the deep peace about them that my presence as a recorder was now unnecessary and entirely out of place. There would be no more to write. The story was done. The prisoner from the Shadows was free. All was in order, as it was meant to be. From now on, my visitors were to pass out of my life, except as memories and characters in a book. But, as I stood bidding them Godspeed in their progress into light, I was glad and thankful for all that had been accomplished, and for the glimpses I had been given of the working of love in the life beyond death.

Slowly a ray of sunshine crept across the window, with a quiver in the beams, and as I watched, the figures faded into the light, and I was alone.

But in the cottage, the atmosphere was stirred, as if a presence had hallowed it . . . as indeed it had!

* * *

The book is finished; the recording is completed; the story is told; the prisoners of self are released, and I am free of my task. It has taken a year and a half in earth time to listen to, to record, and to live *with* these entities; and during that space of time it has made powerful demands on my emotional and spiritual life. As I now emerge and take stock of these happenings, I get a strange feeling that I have made a long sojourn 'in the wilderness'. This has been a difficult period of much trial on many levels. Thankfully, I realise that peace is now restored in my cottage, as in my mind and soul, bringing a new joy and a wider awareness. For, again and again, whilst I am reading, listening to music, or watching television, a closeness with the Spirit pervades my being, and I become aware of a love that holds me, *becomes me*, so that the Self in me is swept into the Eternal. Nothing happens. There is silence and communion. But it is greater than speech, deeper than comfort, higher than aspiration. It is a living flame in the heart, the flame of the undying Spirit in man, in which we are all united, here and in the Beyond.

It is the reality of One-ness; unity with all here on this earth, and in the worlds to come; whether in the Land of the Shadows, in the World of Astral Consciousness, or in the shining Realms of the Spirit.